NATIONAL IMAGES AND UNITED STATES–CANADA RELATIONS

This book explores the psychological–cultural dimension of the United States–Canada relationship by analyzing how each country has viewed the other. Drawing on a wide range of data, including primary sources, secondary literature, and survey research, the methodology is historical/analytical, seeking to explicate and understand how Americans and Canadians, and their elites, have viewed one another from the moment they were launched on separate trajectories, why they developed and held such ideas, and what consequences these images had for the bilateral relationship between the countries. American and Canadian images of the other have deep roots and are, in many respects, recognizably the same today as they were many decades ago. Moreover, even when anchored to important realities of the other, such images influence the perception and interpretation of events, and actions taken by the other. How Americans and Canadians have viewed each other, the sources of these ideas, the way they have been influenced by each country's domestic politics and place within the international system, and the consequences for their bilateral relationship are among the questions examined. Interdisciplinary in approach, the book will appeal to scholars and students of political science, international relations, and history.

Stephen Brooks is a professor at the University of Windsor, Canada. His research focuses on Canadian politics, American politics, and American foreign policy. His publications include *As Others See Us: The Causes and Consequences of Foreign Perceptions of America* (University of Toronto Press, 2006), *American Exceptionalism in the Age of Obama* (Routledge, 2013), and *Anti-Americanism and the Limits of Public Diplomacy: Winning Hearts and Minds* (Routledge, 2016).

InterAmerican Research: Contact, Communication, Conflict
Series Editors
Olaf Kaltmeier, Wilfried Raussert and Sebastian Thies

The Americas are shaped by a multitude of dynamics which have extensive, conflictive and at times contradictory consequences for society, culture, politics and the environment. These processes are embedded within a history of interdependence and mutual observation between North and South which originates in the conquest and simultaneous 'invention' of America by European colonial powers.

The series will challenge the ways we think about the Americas, in particular, and the concept of area studies, in general. Put simply, the series perceives the Americas as transversally related, chronotopically entangled and multiply interconnected. In its critical positioning at the crossroads of area studies and cultural studies the series aims to push further the postcolonial, postnational, and cross-border turns in recent studies of the Americas toward a model of horizontal dialogue between cultures, areas, and disciplines.

The series pursues the goal to 'think the Americas different' and to explore these phenomena from transregional as well as interdisciplinary perspectives.

Sonic Politics
Music and Social Movements in the Americas
Edited by Olaf Kaltmeier and Wilfried Raussert

Human Rights in the Americas
Edited by María Herrera-Sobek, Francisco A. Lomelí and Luz Angélica Kirschner

National Images and United States–Canada Relations
Stephen Brooks

For more information about this series, please visit www.routledge.com/InterAmerican-Research-Contact-Communication-Conflict/book-series/ASHSER-1426

NATIONAL IMAGES AND UNITED STATES–CANADA RELATIONS

Stephen Brooks

LONDON AND NEW YORK

Designed cover image: © Getty Images

First published 2024
by Routledge
4 Park Square, Milton Park, Abingdon, Oxon OX14 4RN

and by Routledge
605 Third Avenue, New York, NY 10158

Routledge is an imprint of the Taylor & Francis Group, an informa business

© 2024 Stephen Brooks

The right of Stephen Brooks to be identified as author of this work has been asserted in accordance with sections 77 and 78 of the Copyright, Designs and Patents Act 1988.

All rights reserved. No part of this book may be reprinted or reproduced or utilised in any form or by any electronic, mechanical, or other means, now known or hereafter invented, including photocopying and recording, or in any information storage or retrieval system, without permission in writing from the publishers.

Trademark notice: Product or corporate names may be trademarks or registered trademarks, and are used only for identification and explanation without intent to infringe.

British Library Cataloguing-in-Publication Data
A catalogue record for this book is available from the British Library

ISBN: 978-1-032-67520-6 (hbk)
ISBN: 978-1-032-67521-3 (pbk)
ISBN: 978-1-032-67522-0 (ebk)

DOI: 10.4324/9781032675220

Typeset in Times New Roman
by Apex CoVantage, LLC

CONTENTS

Acknowledgments vii

1 Images of the Other and International Relations 1

   Introduction: Imagining the Other 1
   When and How Do Images of the Other Matter? 8
   Borderlands: Does Physical Contiguity Make a
      Difference? 16
   National Images and United States–Canada Relations 19

2 America: A Canadian Obsession 22

   Introduction 22
   Early Perceptions: Anti-American Elites and an
      Unconvinced Public 23
   The Rebellions of 1837–38: Rejection of the American
      Model? 31
   Fears of Annexation 34
   Canadian Ambivalence Toward America 37
   The "New" Canadian Nationalism 41
   Multiculturalism as a Marker of Difference
      (and Superiority!) 45
   Old Cultural Tropes Die Hard 47
   American Decline, the Rise of Trumpism, and Canadians'
      Image of America 52
   Conclusion 56

3 Canada: From Existential Threat to the Unknown Country   58

Introduction 58
The Threat From the North 59
*The Early American Image of Les Canadiens
  and the Canadian People 63*
Canada as a Refuge From Injustice 69
Reciprocity and Annexation 71
The Friendly Neighbor Next Door 74
*The Popular Image of Canada: Public Opinion and the
  Media 78*
Canada in America's Culture Wars 80
Conclusion 84

4 A Story of Asymmetry: The Policy Consequences
   of National Images   86

Introduction 86
Economics 87
Security and Defense 88
Communication and Culture 89
The One-Way Mirror 90
The Modern Era in US–Canada Relations 90
Cultural Nationalism in Canada 94
Economic Nationalism in Canada 96
United States–Canada Free Trade 101
The War in Iraq 105
National Images Matter . . . Within Limits 108

References   *114*
Index   *129*

ACKNOWLEDGMENTS

The seeds for this book were planted in Kenneth D. McRae's graduate seminar on Canadian and American Political Thought, taught at Carleton University in 1980–81. That it has taken this long for them to bear fruit has nothing to do with the quality of the seeds nor the skill of the sower. McRae was an exceptional scholar and an inspiring teacher. His insights into the ways in which Americans and Canadians have viewed themselves and their respective societies, and each other, made a profound impression on me.

But the sower's work might well have come to nought had it not been for David M. Thomas, who invited me to contribute a chapter on images of the other and United States–Canada relations for his book, *Canada and the United States: Differences That Count*, now in its 5th edition. At some point, he suggested that I should think about writing a book on the subject. He also made extensive and invariably helpful comments on the manuscript. So in an important way, David Thomas is responsible for the fact that the seeds planted by Kenneth McRae finally bore fruit.

Much can happen between the planting and the harvest. I take sole responsibility for whatever imperfections readers may find in the fruit.

Stephen Brooks
University of Windsor, Canada

1
IMAGES OF THE OTHER AND INTERNATIONAL RELATIONS

Introduction: Imagining the Other

On March 25, 2003, six days after the beginning of the American-led invasion of Iraq, the US Ambassador to Canada, Paul Cellucci, gave a speech in Toronto. In terms that many judged to be undiplomatic or worse, he expressed his government's consternation and disappointment over the Canadian government's decision not to join the Anglo-American coalition of countries supporting military force to remove Saddam Hussein from power. "There is no security threat to Canada that the United States would not be ready, willing, and able to help with. . . . There would be no hesitation. We would be there for Canada, part of our family" (Cellucci 2003).

Cellucci was not simply delivering a message that his government wanted Canadians to hear. The analogy of one family member letting down another in an hour of need was his, and the sense of hurt that accompanied his words was genuine. While he understood the ambivalent feelings that many Canadians and their leaders had when it came to their southern neighbor, Cellucci was nevertheless surprised by the Canadian government's decision and irked by Prime Minister Chrétien's apparent unwillingness to rein in members of his cabinet who were publicly critical of the invasion and of President Bush.[1]

The Chretien government's decision had much to do with the Canadian image of America, or at least the image held by certain parts of the Canadian population and by some of their elites. From Ambassador Cellucci's side, his sincere bafflement and disappointment were grounded on his image of Canada or, more precisely, of Canada's relationship to the United States. He was not alone in assuming that the relationship between the two countries was such that the Canadian government, despite some misgivings, ultimately would support the United States as part of the "Coalition of the Willing." On both sides of the border, the image of the other that influenced the expectations and behavior of their respective governments was based on deeply rooted beliefs and sentiments.

These images already began to emerge when the American War of Independence (1775–83) created a rift between the colonies of British North America. Thirteen of them chose to declare their independence from British rule. Four of the other five would eventually become Canada.[2] The circumstances of their separation and their respective relationships to Britain would be major determinants of how each saw the other for several decades after American independence was achieved. Over time, however, each country's internal development, including its demography, economy and culture, its position in and idea of itself in the wider world, and the nature of its relations with its neighbor, would become the key drivers of how that neighbor was viewed.

This last factor, relations with the other, has been of overriding importance in shaping Canadians' image of the United States and its people. Americans, however, have devoted far less thought to their country's relations with Canada, notwithstanding the scale and intimacy of these ties, and may fairly be said to have taken the relationship for granted much, if not most of the time. This difference reflects the tremendous asymmetry in the US–Canada relationship, a lopsidedness that has often led to resentment on the part of Canadians and surprise, puzzlement, and sometimes annoyance among Americans at what has often been interpreted as the "hyper-sensitivity" of Canadians and their governments (Doran and Sewell 1988).

The images that populations have of one another are only one determinant of their bilateral relations. Most of the time, at least in a proximate sense, it is not the most important one in its influence on a particular issue or even on the general character of their relations. These images can and often do, however, operate as a sort of interpretative filter through which the actions and motives of the other are perceived. At the most profound level, a nation's image of the other may be grounded on historical memory, as between Germany and France, France and England, Ireland and England, Croatians and Serbs, Turks and Greeks, Iran and the United States, and many other international dyads that immediately come to mind. Those who study national images and the historical memories on which they are based know them to be remarkably durable and resistant to contradiction (Fält 1995).

This durability may be based on historical facts or, at least, beliefs that are widely accepted as factually based. If Poles have long mistrusted Russia and its rulers, believing them to be expansionist and threatening to Polish territory and independence, the fact that for most of the past three centuries, Russia has occupied and controlled all of what is currently the state of Poland – a historical fact – is part of the reason for this long-standing and deep mistrust. Some of the longest held and most durable beliefs that one population has about another have to do with histories of conflict, rivalry, or antagonism of some sort.

The durability of such beliefs does not depend on a factual basis and, indeed, they often prove to be quite impervious to challenges based on what we might think of as facts. In *The Righteous Mind: Why Good People Are Divided by Politics and Religion*,

Images of the Other and International Relations 3

"What part of Canada that I know nothing about are you from?"

FIGURE 1.1 Despite sharing the world's longest international border and about 250 years of history, to say nothing of the dense network of linkages that connect the United States and Canada, Americans typically know very little about their northern neighbor.

Photograph by Liam Walsh. Reproduced with permission.

Jonathan Haidt concludes that "our minds were designed for groupish righteousness. We are deeply intuitive creatures whose gut feelings drive our strategic reasoning" (Haidt 2012, 370). The scientific literature on prejudice and in-group bias supports this view on the role played by stereotypes and irrationality in the construction and reproduction of images of the other (Cuddy et al. 2007; Dovidio et al. 2010).

Historical facts can also nurture national images that prove to be durable over time. Facts, however, may be complicated things and subject to interpretation. The majority of Americans believe that the terrorist attacks of September 11, 2001, were orchestrated by Al-Qaeda under the direction of Osama bin Laden, carried out by people who were Muslims, and that they resulted in thousands of deaths, including many Jews. Majorities in all western societies accept these facts. But a 2007 Zogby survey found that about one-quarter of Americans believed that "certain US government elements actively planned or assisted some aspects of the attacks" (Zogby 2007). Seven years later, a 2014 Rasmussen poll found that about one in four Americans believed that 9/11 was somehow an "inside job," perpetrated by their own government. This belief is about equally likely to be held by Democrats as Republicans (Enders et al. 2020). Significant minorities in other western democracies, greater than a quarter of the population in some cases, agreed. Even among those who accept that the facts are that the United States was attacked by Islamist terrorists, the interpretation of these facts varies dramatically. The vast majority of Americans see their country as the victim of an unjust attack. But some Americans and a considerably larger share of persons in other western societies believe that the United States had it coming. For them, America was not the victim, or at least was no more a victim than those countries and peoples that the United States had victimized in its turn.

What determines whether, first, one believes that the attacks of 9/11 were the work of Islamist terrorists or an inside job and, second, whether one sees the America as the victim of an unjustified act? The answer is what one believed about America *before* the attacks took place. It is virtually certain that for the majority of people, the events of 9/11 provided corroboration of already existing images and beliefs.

The power of confirmation bias is well known. Despite this, many astute and well-respected commentators expressed shock and incredulity that so many people, in America but particularly abroad, purported to believe that 9/11 was the handiwork of the CIA, the Mossad, international Jewry, the Trilateral Commission, or some combination of shadowy forces pulling the strings in a *poppenspiel* of global domination. In fact, however, this is exactly what should have been expected. As Kenneth Boulding writes,

> The image [of a nation] is always in some sense a product of messages received in the past . . . [It is] a highly structured piece of information-capital, developed partly by its inputs and outputs of information and partly by internal messages and its own laws of growth and stability.
>
> *(Boulding 1959, 121)*

Boulding's analysis of the role played by national images in international systems was written during the Cold War, at that particularly tense moment in history between the launch of the Sputnik satellite and the Cuban Missile Crisis. "[W]e live in an international system so unstable that it threatens the very existence of life on earth," he wrote. Much of the reason for the extraordinary level of tension in geopolitics, Boulding argued, involved the images that powerful nations had of each other. "The national image is the last great stronghold of unsophistication," he declared, adding that "the ordinary citizen and the powerful statesman alike have naïve, self-centered, and unsophisticated images of the world in which their nation moves" (Boulding 1959, 131).[3]

Boulding was guardedly optimistic that it is possible, in democracies at least, to overcome what he characterized as a lack of sophistication in how nations and geopolitical forces are viewed. By sophistication, he meant the capacity to view the world "from many imagined viewpoints, as a system in which the viewer is only a part" (Boulding 1959, 130). In this direction, he believed, lies salvation from the animosities, misunderstandings, and conflicts whose roots may be found in a failure to see other nations and one's own in ways that are not merely or even chiefly the products of accumulated ideas, familiar stereotypes, and inherited narratives.

Neither the literature on the formation and functions of national images nor the historical record provides much cause for optimism that these images may be easily or quickly changed. Indeed, in his 1957 book, *The Image: Knowledge in Life and Society*, Boulding examined the roots of these national images in formative life experiences and early learning and emphasized their resistance to change (Boulding 1957). The first and perhaps still the seminal work on this subject, Walter Lippmann's *Public Opinion*, also stressed the durability of ideas, beliefs, and stereotypes when it comes to peoples and events that lie far from a person's immediate circle of experience. Much of the field of cognitive psychology is devoted to explaining why ideas, images, and dispositions acquired early in one's life are, generally speaking, highly resistant to change. The literature on how national populations perceive others is virtually unanimous in concluding that the most remarkable characteristic of such perceptions is their durability. Indeed, as Olavi Fält writes,

> it is typical of an image that though it may change from a negative one to a positive one its negative aspects do not disappear but are merely no longer visible on the surface. They are in fact still there "in the cellar," gathering dust but nevertheless fresh and ready to emerge.
>
> *(Fält 1995, 104)*

Examples of this emergence from the cellar are not hard to come by. During the European debt crisis, leading up to a second EU bailout of Greece in March of 2012, many German leaders and the preponderance of German public opinion were opposed to continued financial support for Greece without much more draconian measures being taken by the Greek government to rein in spending and reduce public sector debt. In Greece, the German government of Angela Merkel was compared to the Nazis who had occupied Greece during World War II. In street posters and political cartoons, Merkel, her finance minister Wolfgang Schäuble, and German officials more generally were portrayed in Nazi uniforms (Ferris-Rotman 2011). In 2015, when it appeared that Greece might default on the bailout money that it had received, the country's finance minister, Yanis Varoufakis, put a rather different twist on the Nazi comparison. "If you humiliate a proud nation for too long," he said, in an obvious reference to post-Versailles Germany, "and subject it to the worry of a debt deflation crisis, without light at the end of a tunnel then things come to the boil" (quoted in BBC 2015).

Events and prominent persons from a country's past may provide the basis for the image that others have of a nation, its leaders, and its actions. Even before the

Russian annexation of Crimea in 2014 and its 2022 invasion of Ukraine, comparisons of President Vladimir Putin to Joseph Stalin were commonplace in the media of western and eastern Europe and in North America. Several national leaders joined in, including those of Finland, Poland, and Lithuania, countries that had experience of Russian (then, the Soviet Union) occupation under Stalin. The issue is not whether such a comparison is accurate. Rather, the point is that it comes naturally in countries whose histories include fraught relations with Russia long before Putin and even before Stalin.

Relations between the United States and Iran provide yet another example of how sentiments and beliefs that have been in the cellar may easily resurface. Indeed, in this case, it may even be too much to say that Iranian mistrust of the United States has been in the cellar at any point since the CIA assisted in the 1953 coup that brought down the government of Prime Minister Mohammad Mosaddegh. American involvement in the coup and support of the Shah's repressive regime in the decades that followed continue to be pointed to as proof of the perfidious and untrustworthy motives of the US government, a view that is widely shared even by those who are otherwise not enamored of the theocracy that rules Iran (Datta 2020).

Indeed, it may well be that the populations and leaders of more countries have ideas and sentiments "in the cellar" concerning America than is true of any other country. The list is a long one. It includes Mexico and, indeed, Latin America generally. Mexico's loss of half its territory to the United States in the mid-1800s, and widespread resentment across Latin America toward what has been seen as America's history of imperialism across the region, continues to fuel anti-American sentiment and suspicion of the US government's motives. Canada is also on this list of countries. As we will see in Chapter 2, some of the widely held tropes and deep-seated beliefs held by Canadians about America have their roots in the early decades of a relationship that is now roughly 250 years old. Ideas about America are even older in the case of Europe. In his book, *Uncouth Nation*, Andrei Markovits argues that much of what one finds in contemporary European ideas about the United States may be traced back over three hundred years to the rather negative interpretations and images of America constructed by many European intellectuals and political leaders (Markovits 2007).

Of course, this works both ways. Americans have been no less likely than other peoples to have long-standing and durable images of at least some countries, regions, and peoples. Indeed, considerable literatures exist on American images of Russia, China, and Islam, to mention a few images of the other that have been prominent in recent decades (United States 1978; Zimmerman 1977; Isaacs 1972; Cohen 1973; Sherrard, undated). Canada has received less attention in this respect, except viewed from the angle of US–Canada comparisons of political culture, institutions, social behavior, and public policies. Moreover, these national images have often been an important factor in shaping American foreign policies.

Perhaps the best-known instance of this influence involves the image of the Russian people and of the Soviet elite that George Kennan provided in his 1946

"Long Telegram" from Moscow to the Secretary of State. In his long briefing note, Kennan describes and interprets what he calls the "post-war Soviet outlook" and "the background of this outlook" (Kennan 1945). His thinking had an important influence on the American policy of containment during the decades following World War II. More recently, Rumer and Sokolsky, among others, have argued that American policy toward Russia since the break-up of the Soviet Union has been based on serious misperceptions regarding the Russian outlook, and particularly of its ruling elite, in matters of national security, and how this outlook is rooted in the long history of the country's often antagonistic relations with its neighbors (Rumer and Sokolsky 2021).

Rumer and Sokolsky call these mistaken and uninformed ideas about the Russian outlook, "grand illusions." They might be of little consequence if those who shape the conversation on American foreign policy and those who make and implement it did not subscribe to them. It is probably reasonable to assume that members of the foreign policy elite are, on the whole and most of the time, better informed about international affairs and the cultures and histories of countries with which America has relations than is true of the general population. Moreover, most studies of the impact of public opinion on American foreign policy conclude that, most of the time, the ideas and images of elites count for more than those of the general public (Foyle 1997; Holsti 2004). Nevertheless, not all of those who influence the conversation on America's foreign relations and those who have their hands near the levers of policy-making on such matters are well-informed when it comes to their understanding of other countries and peoples, nor are they all of the same mind when it comes to how they perceive other countries. Based on interviews with 181 "American policy makers and opinion shapers . . . all individuals occupying key places in the communications network of the society," Harold Isaacs reached this conclusion:

> [A]n individual's perceptions of another people and another culture are shaped and colored by his own particular window on the world: the time, place and circumstances of the encounter, his particular background and education, the elements of his own unique personality . . . and the political conditions, the power relations, existing at the time when these ideas were fixed in his mind. . . . [T]he best-schooled minds are embarrassingly capable of carrying the most flagrant prejudices and stereotypes . . . and [these] can be held firmly over the years, even a whole lifetime, without ever coming under critical examination.
> *(Isaacs 1970, 95–96)*

Isaac's study was carried out in the mid-1950s. One might argue that American opinion-leaders and policy-makers in our times are less likely to be ill-informed and to engage the sort of stereotyped thinking that Isaac found to be not uncommon among his interviewees. His study has not been replicated over the years, so it is hard to know how its conclusions would stand up today. What we do know with some certainty, however, is that there are wide divergences among contemporary foreign policy opinion-leaders and politicians when it comes to their beliefs about other countries, regions, and peoples of the world. Even cursory attention to the ideas, images, and arguments that are aired in the media and that presumably have some influence – even if it is just the confirmation of the pre-existing views of those who read, see, and hear them – suggests that Isaac's observation that "the best-schooled minds are embarrassingly capable of carrying the most flagrant prejudices and stereotypes," is probably as true today as when he made it.

This certainly is true of the ideas and images that Canadians and Americans, and many of their leaders, have about each other. With the notable exception of a rather devout and intrepid cadre of Canadianists in the United States, serious knowledge about or even interest in Canada is quite uncommon. It is revealing that when William Buchanan and Hadley Cantril chose the list of countries that would be included in their UNESCO-sponsored study of "the conceptions which the people of one nation entertain of their own and other nations" (Buchanan and Cantril 1953, v), undertaken in 1948–49, Canada was not included nor even contemplated for inclusion in a cross-national survey that included Australia, Britain, France, Germany, Italy, the Netherlands, Norway, Mexico, and the United States. Countries that were considered for study but not included for various reasons included Belgium, China, a major South American country, Hungary, and Czechoslovakia (Buchanan and Cantril 1953, vi–vii). It was very likely the case, already at this moment in time, that it did not occur to these two American scholars that Canada was a "foreign" country as this was understood within the unstated parameters of their research project.

From the Canadian side, however, interest in the United States has long been a given of the national condition. Moreover, there is no doubt that Canadians and their leaders have been and continue to be more much knowledgeable when it comes to the United States than Americans are of Canada. This does not mean, however, that what they believe about their neighbor is free of stereotypes and prejudices and usually well-informed. Isaac's warning about education not being a guarantee of greater clarity and fairness in one's view of the other applies to Canada as well.

When and How Do Images of the Other Matter?

The national image of a country may be an asset or a liability in international relations. It certainly can influence how citizens and their leaders react to what are believed to be the actions, words, and motives of another nation and its government. This, at least, is the conclusion reached by many who study the impact of national images on the relations between countries and peoples (Nye 2004). It is also agreed by state elites in many countries of the world, whose attempts to cultivate and maintain a favorable image abroad have been motivated by the belief that this will make a difference in their country's ability to achieve some of its foreign policy goals. Democratic and non-democratic regimes alike have invested considerable money and effort in order to project a particular image and to persuade at least some foreign audiences that this image is an accurate likeness of their country, its values, and its achievements.

A nation's image is widely believed to be an important and impactful aspect of its soft power. The term "soft power" is defined by Joseph Nye as a nation's ability to attract others to follow its example and to want conditions and outcomes that are desired by that nation. It may rest on approval and admiration of a nation's values, institutions, economic or other accomplishments, or on some combination of factors that convince and persuade rather than frighten and threaten. Nye goes so far as to refer to it as "the means to success in world politics," the subtitle of his 2004 book, *Soft Power*. While he is widely credited for having coined the term, the idea of soft power is a very old one. Indeed, Nye acknowledges this at the beginning of *Soft Power*, where he writes, "Niccolo Machiavelli advised princes in Italy that it was more important to be feared than to be loved. But in today's world, it is best to be both" (Nye 2004, 1). Two millennia before Machiavelli, Thucydides – who, like Machiavelli, is also associated with the view that hard power and fear provide a firmer foundation for national influence than admiration – made the case that the image that other states held of Athens was an important pillar on which the legitimacy that others ascribed to its hegemony rested. When admiration for Athens waned, due to actions of its leaders that undermined the legitimacy of its dominance, so too did its influence in the Mediterranean world (Lebow and Kelly 2001).

Americans and their leaders have long believed in the importance of their nation's image and seen in it a source of their country's influence in the world. This was so long before their country's economic or military power on the world stage provided a hard power basis for such influence. The fledgling nation's self-image was first expressed in 1630 by John Winthrop, the governor of the Massachusetts Bay Colony, who famously predicted, "We shall be as a city upon a hill. The eyes of all people are upon us" (Winthrop 1630). The image that many Americans and their leaders had of their nation's role in the world and in world history would be central to the revolution against British rule. The second paragraph of the Declaration of Independence is well known to all students of American history, but it is in the first paragraph that Thomas Jefferson makes clear that he is addressing the world and generations yet to come. Announcing the independence of the United States, he writes that "a decent respect to the *opinions of mankind requires* that they should declare the causes which impel them to the separation" (emphasis added). Jefferson, Thomas Paine, Benjamin Franklin, James Madison, George Washington, and other leading figures of the revolutionary era believed that they were making history by creating a model of society and politics in accordance with enlightenment ideas of popular sovereignty and the natural right of persons to equality and freedom. They also believed that the attractions of what would often be referred to as the American system would be found irresistible by peoples throughout the world.

Many Europeans agreed, some fearing this prospect and others welcoming it (Fairlie 1988). Whatever their views, elites and the literate classes in Europe were aware of the revolutionary ideology and the associated system of government that was the first influential projection abroad of what might be described as America's national image. "[T]his government, the world's best hope," as Jefferson put it in his 1801 inaugural address, was an article of faith among all of the leading statesmen in the early decades of the Republic. They also believed that the United States was destined to rival and then surpass Europe in economic and military power, differing only in estimates of how long this might take. But even before this day would be reached, they believed in the influence of the model that they presented to the world and were confident that other peoples – particularly not only those who had been colonized by European powers but also those who lived under political and social systems that denied to them the rights of man expounded in the Declaration of Independence – would want the same. They were the first in a long line of American leaders to recognize that their country's influence in the world rested in no small measure on soft power.

Recognition and action were two different things. When the American state took deliberate steps to project a particular image abroad, it was through recruitment posters, newspaper ads, pamphlets, maps, and other literature that attempted to persuade Europeans to immigrate to the United States. Most of these recruitment efforts, and the accompanying images of affordable land and the promise of prosperity, were launched by state governments. Railroad companies, steamship lines, and even some faith communities were also active in projecting what they hoped would be an attractive image of America, or at least a particular part of the country, in order to persuade farmers and working-class Europeans to emigrate (Curti and Birr 1950).

It was not until the middle of the 20th century, however, that the American government would take a systematic approach toward its national image abroad. Spurred by the Cold War with the Soviet Union and what quickly became a struggle for the hearts and minds of populations throughout the world, Congress passed laws creating the Voice of America (1942),[4] the Fulbright Program (1946), Radio Free Europe (1949), the United States Information Agency (1953), and the Peace Corps (1961). Beginning with President Kennedy's 1961 speech at the Brandenburg Gate in Berlin, presidential visits abroad became an important feature of American public diplomacy. The persuasiveness of these efforts to shape the image held of the United States by foreign audiences has sometimes seemed doubtful. Nevertheless, they have been an important tool of foreign policy since World War II.

The national image of the United States has never, however, depended on the efforts of the American state. More important have been the unorchestrated actions of individuals and organizations who have been seen as representative of American values and goals. The thousands of missionaries who went abroad, beginning as early as 1812, were doubtless seen as the carriers of American values and ideas. Their numbers were dwarfed by the emissaries of American business, who carried American commerce to the shores of other countries and brought with them their language, mores, and manners. But possibly more important than Americans who traveled abroad for religious or commercial reasons, and more important than the state's recruitment efforts during the 19th century, were the impressions of America communicated to foreigners by those who had already immigrated to America. "Most immigrants," write Curti and Birr,

> listened to the voices of friends and neighbors who had emigrated before them. Most contemporary observers and subsequent investigators have agreed upon that. A comparison of immigration statistics and postal statistics reveals considerable correspondence between the immigration from a specific country and the weight of the mails sent there.
>
> *(212–213)*

The image of America that was conveyed by the state, private companies, and in the letters sent home by immigrants was, in the main, summed up in a song that appears to have been very popular in Great Britain during the mid-19th century and that encouraged the father of Andrew Carnegie to emigrate. It opens with these words,

> To the west, to the west, to the land of the free
> Where mighty Missouri rolls down to the sea;
> Where a man is a man if he's willing to toil,
> And the humblest may gather the fruits of the soil.
> Where children are blessings and he who hath most
> Has aid for his fortune and riches to boast.
> (Mackay 1876, 549)

It is impossible to determine with any certainty the relative importance of the various sources that have contributed over the years to foreigners' image of America. There is little doubt, however, of the primacy of film. With the advent of cinema and the rapid ascendance of Hollywood as the center of this industry, the images and ideas conveyed by print receded into the background. Both Jean-Paul Sartre and Simone de Beauvoir, famous for their anti-Americanism, acknowledge the influence that the American films they watched in France had on their respective images of America.[5] In this respect, at least, they were no different from millions of their French compatriots. It appears that only protectionist measures imposed by the French government in the late 1920s kept American films from being even more popular than they were in that country's cinemas. Even so, they never fell below about 40 percent of total box office revenues (Bakker, undated).

The penetration and domination of American films in many other foreign markets would be even greater. Interestingly, until quite recently the success of a film in the American domestic market was a strong predictor of its success in foreign markets (Miskell 2014). The explanation for this correlation is a matter of conjecture. One possibility, offered by Richard Maltby, is that "the 'America' of the movies has presented itself to its audiences less as a geographical territory than an imaginative one, which deliberately made itself available for assimilation in a variety of cultural contexts" (Maltby 2004, 4). The apparent decline in this correlation in more recent years, according to some analysts, has the same cause. Hollywood studios, recognizing the growing importance of foreign markets, have continued to make their films "universal," but in ways that may appeal less to American audiences (Mirrlees 2018).

Increasingly, the national image of America is as likely to be shaped by what foreign audiences consume on the small screen as on the big screen. This may not diminish, however, the impact of Hollywood and the American entertainment and celebrity industries more generally, on what foreign populations believe about American ideas, institutions, manners, and America's impact on the rest of the world. The accounts of American celebrities dominate Instagram, TikTok, YouTube, Facebook, WhatsApp, and other social media platforms. Beyond the communication of celebrity culture, there are reasons to believe that the worldwide growth of social media has also promoted the export of some aspects of American political culture (The Economist 2021).

The idea that their national image might matter came later to Canadians than to Americans. When it did, it was in the late 19th century as a state-directed project to

FIGURE 1.2 This image is from a 1903 Canadian government pamphlet that aimed to attract immigrants to Canada's prairies. The accompanying text included the following images contrasting conditions in the United States and Canada: "They were coming to 'the land that produced the finest of the wheat' – where cyclones are unknown, where the crops show large and profitable yields, and where civil rights and religious liberty are maintained and enjoyed."

Image from: "Canada, the granary of the world." Government of Canada, Department of the Interior, 1903. Peel's Prairie Provinces, University of Alberta Libraries.

encourage European immigrants to settle in the sparsely populated western regions of the country. "Own your own home in Canada," "The Last Best West," "The New Eldorado," and "Canada – The New Homeland" were among the poster inscriptions, accompanied by images of open, prosperous, healthy spaces. In addition to posters, government-sponsored lectures were organized, particularly in the United Kingdom. These recruitment efforts also targeted eastern Europe and the Scandinavian countries, as well as the United States (Canadian Museum of History, undated). As was also true of American recruitment campaigns during this era, government efforts were joined by those of railroad companies and steamship lines, all promising the dream of a bright new future and independence in the New World (Library and Archives Canada 2017).

The optimism projected by these attempts to sell the idea of a future in Canada to prospective immigrants may be sensed in the prime minister's famous promise made during the 1904 federal election campaign:

> I assert that the name of Canada during [the past 8 years of my government] has traveled far and wide and whether a man be a friend or be a foe, he knows he must admit that there are today in Europe thousands and thousands of men who had never heard the name Canada eight years ago, and who today, every day, turn their eyes toward this new star which has appeared in the western sky . . .
>
> I tell you that the nineteenth century has been the century of United States development. The past 100 years has been filled with the pages of their history. Let me tell you, my fellow countrymen, that all the signs point this way, that the twentieth century shall be the century of Canada and of Canadian development. For the next 75 years, nay for the next 100 years, Canada shall be the star towards which all men who love progress and freedom shall come.[6]
>
> *(Laurier 1904)*

The mention of the United States in his promise that Canada would supplant its southern neighbor in the minds and hopes of peoples throughout the world is not surprising. Laurier was not anti-American. But like most of the leading Canadians of his generation – and those since – he was unable to envisage future Canadian greatness without comparison to the country that already had become synonymous with "progress and freedom" in the eyes of many throughout the world, including Canadians.

With the outbreak of World War I, the campaign to attract immigrants largely wound down. Almost nothing further was done by the Canadian government to project the country's image abroad until well into the 20th century. The reason was quite simply that for the first half-century of its existence, Canada did not have constitutional authority over its relations with other countries. This remained formally under British control until 1926. Until then, Canada had diplomatic representation in only London, beginning in 1880 with the establishment of its High Commission to the

United Kingdom. From 1882, and due only to the actions of the Quebec provincial government, there was a Canadian representative in France who had no formal diplomatic status. It was not until 1944 that a Canadian embassy was established in France. One year earlier, the Canadian embassy in Washington, DC, opened, although formal recognition by the US government of Canada's autonomy in the management of its foreign relations dated from 1926. In short, until the post-World War II era, the Canadian state lacked the institutional means to project an image abroad that was distinct from its status as a member of the British Empire. Indeed, it was not until the passage in 1946 of the *Canadian Citizenship Act* that Canadian nationals were legally described as Canadian citizens rather than as British subjects.

While the Canadian state stood mainly on the sidelines, at least one private organization was busy projecting a national image to markets abroad. The Canadian Pacific Railway was in dire need of passenger traffic from its early beginnings in 1886. Under its president, Cornelius Van Horne and continued under his successor Thomas Shaughnessy, it launched a decades-long campaign at home and abroad, including in Europe and the United States, to attract tourists. As E.J. Hart writes,

> By the 1920s, [the CPR's] tourist operations embraced Canada from coast to coast and spanned the world. For several decades its tourist advertising delineated the view of Canada, both at home and around the world. Its view of Canada as a place of scenic wonders and cultural diversity prevails even to this day.
> *(Hart 1983, 7)*

Indeed, the poster art that was commissioned by the CPR in the early 20th century included iconic images that helped cement in the imagination of Canadians and non-Canadians alike, a national image that featured a few people and cities, but many mountains and forests, and much wildlife.

By the mid-20th century, the national image of Canada did not extend very far beyond the CPR poster art and similar portrayals that emphasized vastness and natural beauty. Even among Canadians, the image they held of their country did not stress its history, values, and institutions. One of the foremost Canadian historians of his generation, A.R.M. Lower, complained about his compatriots that "[f]ew people read any history and fewer still read any Canadian history. Relatively few are interested in Canada" (Lower 1953, x–xi). Indeed, until after World War II, very few Canadian universities offered a single course in Canadian history. Indeed, more such courses were offered in the United States – generally taught by professors of Canadian origin – than in Canada (Berger 1972).

If Canadians (English Canadians, at least) were rather uncertain when it came to their national image, it was unsurprising that they were not seen in sharper focus by their American neighbors. Writing in 1952, at a moment in time when Canada had clearly passed from the British Empire into the orbit of the new American imperium, Richard W. Van Alstyne observed, "Canada, the second ranking nation of the American continent and the one closest in every respect to the United States, draws only a blank in the minds of most educated Americans" (Van Alstyne 1952, 280). Generally speaking, this ignorance and indifference, benign as it was, generated resentment among most Canadians.

When the Canadian state turned its attention to the country's image abroad, during the 1960s, it was due to serendipity and the entrepreneurship of Montreal's mayor, Jean Drapeau. In 1960, Moscow had been awarded the right to host the 1967 World Exposition, Canada's bid finishing second. Two years later, the Soviet Union announced that it would not organize the exposition. Neither the Canadian government nor the leader of the major opposition party appeared particularly interested in resubmitting Canada's bid, doing so mainly because of the persistence of Montreal's mayor. As it happened, 1967 was also the centenary of Canadian confederation. Although the celebration of Canada's centennial year and the World Exposition would take place in the same year, the latter was not formally part of the centenary celebrations. Nevertheless, it was seen by most Canadians to be the crowning event of Canada's centennial year, a perception that has persisted down to the present day (Davies 1999, Chapter 4).

World expositions, as is also true of the Olympic Games and the World Cup of football, provide the host country with an opportunity to showcase its accomplishments and to project to the world the national image that it wishes viewers and visitors from around the world to take away from the experience. The image projected at Expo 67 was modernistic and oriented toward future possibilities rather than a celebration of past accomplishments and traditions. "The international press raved about the Fair," writes Helen Davies,

> with reporters from all over the globe declaring Expo a magnificent success. They praised Canada for hosting an event that was unlike any other World Fair and that did not simply duplicate past European or American examples. According to the media from overseas, Expo gave expression to a uniquely Canadian vision, one that left visitors with the sense that Canada had "grown up."
> *(Davies 1999, 162)*

Of the roughly 64 million visitors to Expo 67, an estimated 45 percent were Americans (Aykroyd 1992, 170). The exposition included pavilions representing 62 countries and, during its six months, it hosted 92 heads of state or heads of government. It was, in short, a national image opportunity on a scale that Canada has never experienced, before or since.

A much smaller, but more sustained effort to make Canada better known on the world stage began in the mid-1970s when the Canadian government began to provide financial support for Canadian studies abroad (Brooks 2019). Along with financial assistance for other forms of cultural diplomacy, such as financing Canadian musical and theatrical performances, and art expositions abroad, this became an officially recognized instrument of Canadian foreign policy for roughly four decades, until the government's 2010 foreign policy review. Cultural diplomacy did not receive a mention in that review and, within a couple of years, the last funding for Canadian studies abroad, most of which went to finance programs, courses, researchers, and events in the United States, dried up. The reaction of the Canadian studies community was summed up by the former director of the Canadian Studies Program at the University of Vermont in the following words: "Canada's image abroad: fade to black" (Martin 2012). Explaining why Duke University, one of the cradles of Canadian studies in the United States, would no longer finance its Canadian program, the Vice-Provost of International Studies asked, "If [Canadian Prime Minister] Stephen Harper doesn't support Canadian studies, why should we?" (Coates 2015). The financing of such programs by the Canadian government has never been restored.

Even during the decades when the Canadian state was active in financing the study of Canada in the United States and in countries across the world, the amounts spent on cultural diplomacy, and on public diplomacy more generally, were miniscule compared to spending by such countries as the United States, the United Kingdom, France, and Japan. Moreover, as Evan Potter argues, such programs have never been part of a strategic and comprehensive approach to the projection of Canada's national image in the United States or in the world more generally[7] (Potter 2009).

Unlike the United States and a handful of other countries in the world, Canada has never been able to rely on its cultural footprint in the world in order to project a national image that goes beyond the usual tropes: it has a vast territory and a relatively small population; it is northern and rather cold for much of the year; it is a wealthy democracy and a rather welcoming place; and it has as its neighbor the world's most powerful country. This may not be problematic when it comes to Canada's relations with Denmark or Ecuador. But it might be useful if Americans and their leaders knew that Canada has been, for decades, the United States' largest source of imported energy, the single largest export destination for over 30 American states and that none of the 9/11 terrorists made their way to the United States through Canada. These are facts that are unknown, not only to most Americans but to many of their politicians and opinion-leaders.

Borderlands: Does Physical Contiguity Make a Difference?

The asymmetry in knowledge about and interest in the other that has long characterized the United States–Canada relationship might be expected to be less in border communities. In such spaces, the ties of trade and the cross-border movement of persons are especially great, the nature of their common interests are perhaps more obvious and likely to be recognized by large numbers of persons on both sides of the border as vital, and demographic or cultural similarities may, for historical reasons, be greater than those that exist between the two countries more generally. The most notable of such cross-border communities include the Great Lakes region, the Pacific Northwest of the United States and the contiguous Pacific

Southwest of Canada, and the region that encompasses New England in the United States and the eastern Canadian provinces of Quebec, New Brunswick, and Nova Scotia. In these cases, perhaps, the images that Americans and their leaders have of their Canadian neighbors may be different from those held by their compatriots further from the border, in ways that make a difference in international relations within these cross-border communities.

This possibility has been recognized by a number of studies on the cross-border communities spanning the international boundary between the United States and Canada. A study of cross-border regions sponsored by the Government of Canada and carried out by Canadian and American researchers concluded that "the existence of commonly held and shared values among business and community leaders on both sides of the border facilitates the creation and expansion of cross-border links, and the development of cross-border regions" (Brunet-Jailly 2006, 6). This research examined the attitudes and beliefs of business and organizational leaders from the two countries, rather than the general populations within the cross-border regions that were studied. Personal and organizational linkages and value affinities at the subnational level were identified as important factors that facilitated economic cooperation and integration within these cross-border communities. Cultural affinities were judged to be much less important to the existence of these communities than economic ties, physical proximity and geography, and shared ecosystems. The issue of how these leaders viewed the other country and its people was not specifically addressed in the North American Linkages project.

There is evidence that cultural affinities connecting contiguous regions in what historian Katherine Morrissey calls "mental territories" have proven to be important in developing and sustaining a shared sense of identity across the US–Canada border and, in the process, contributing to integration. In her study of what was known in the late 1800s and early 1900s as the "Inland Empire," a vast territory encompassing much of the American states of Washington and Idaho and parts of Montana and Oregon, as well as southern regions of the Canadian province of British Columbia, Morrissey writes,

> The boundary at the forty-ninth parallel clearly existed as a political line. . . . In personal accounts, however, individuals noted the environmental and economic lines that bisected the political line. Most important, they emphasized the kinship ties that deflated the border's significance in their lives within the region.
> *(Morrissey 1998, 123)*

This cross-border identity did not accord with the interests of the Canadian state, nor with those of certain Canadian business interests, particularly the Canadian Pacific Railway and Canadian mining companies. "Vigorous efforts were made," Morrissey argues, "to counter the pervasive over-the-border influences" (Morrissey 1998, 129). A mental territory that had emerged organically, without regard or respect for a national border, challenged the nation-building designs of Canadian politicians and the economic interests of some Canadian capitalists.

In their book on the history of the border in the Great Lakes region, John Bukowczyk and his colleagues examine what has been for centuries the most populous US–Canada cross-border community (Bukowczyk et al. 2005). Consisting of the upper Midwest states and Ontario, the image that those on the one side of the international border have had of those on the other has been refracted through an especially dense web of trade, migration, and culture. The authors' focus is, primarily, on the shared history of this borderland region prior to the mid-20th century. The international border was, as they demonstrate, exceptionally permeable, and this may well have contributed to a degree of cultural integration that facilitated cooperation at the subnational level. But as H.V. Nelles observes in his review of this book,

> In some respects as people we have grown apart even as certain aspects of our economies have become integrated well beyond borderland regions. A permeable border perhaps, but it is also permanent; it does separate, and what it separates, changes.
>
> *(Nelles 2007, 139)*

Nelles's insistence on the primacy of the international border as a factor that eventually and inevitably reinforces differences between the American and Canadian populations that it separates may indeed be valid. At the same time, however, studies of public policies and political culture in contiguous regions of the United States and Canada suggest that cultural affinities in such regions may contribute to greater similarities in some public policies than exist between Canadian and American regions that are not contiguous. The relative importance of cultural values, compared to demography, economics, physical geography, and climate, is not clear (Banting et al. 2019; VanNijnatten 2006).

In one of the few survey-based studies of how proximity may affect American and Canadian perceptions of the other, Timothy Gravelle (Gravelle 2014) takes as his theoretical starting point Gordon Allport's work on inter-group contact and prejudice (Allport 1954). Allport's finding that greater contact between the members of groups tends to be associated with more positive feelings between them has been confirmed by many studies. Applying the inter-group contact theory to the views that Canadians and Americans have of each other, Gravelle hypothesizes that closer proximity to the other will be correlated with more positive impressions.

Gravelle finds that border proximity is indeed correlated with attitudes toward the other. The relationship is fairly straightforward in the case of American views of Canada. "[P]roximity to the Canada – US border leads to more favourable attitudes toward Canada, but this effect is most pronounced among Democrats" (Gravelle 2014, 151). In the case of Canadians, however, border proximity has the effect of amplifying positive attitudes toward the United States among those who identify with the Liberal or Conservative parties – Canada's major political parties – but is associated with more negative attitudes among those who identify with the New Democratic Party or the Bloc Québécois (Gravelle 2014, 148).

Gravelle's findings may appear to suggest that, when it comes to issues of concern to contiguous regions of the United States and Canada, the resolution of these matters may be helped by the more positive feelings and more informed understanding of the other that exist in cross-border regions than at the national level. The likelihood that this will be the case depends, however, on whether the key decision-makers are within the cross-border region. But even if the issue is one where the key decision-makers are far from the border in Washington, DC, and Ottawa, as is the case for most matters of shared concern in US–Canada border regions, there remains the possibility that an affinity of views and goodwill at the regional level may influence decision-makers whose image of the other is less informed and perhaps less pre-disposed to be positive.

National Images and United States–Canada Relations

Explanations of US–Canada relations typically point to the importance of factors that are relatively easy to measure, or at least to observe. They include economic linkages between the two countries, the movement of goods, capital, and people between them, infrastructure that spans the border, and some aspects of their shared geography and ecosystems. Institutional and legal ties between them, including treaties, membership in bilateral and multilateral organizations, and business, environmental, and other associations that include members from both sides of the border also fall into this category. To this, we might add attitudes and beliefs, as these are measured by public opinion surveys, or gleaned from the media or pronouncements of opinion-leaders in the United States and Canada, respectively.

The image that each population and its leaders hold of the other country is something that can be measured using opinion surveys and intuited from how the other is depicted in the media and in the words of opinion-leaders. In fact, however, beyond questions that attempt to gauge in the most general manner Americans' feelings toward Canada and Canadians, and those of Canadians toward their northern neighbor, very little survey data exists when it comes to these national images. Such measures are interesting and certainly tell us something important about the temperature of the relationship between the United States and Canada. They may be less useful in helping to explain why particular aspects of the bilateral relationship unfold as they do.

There is, however, an abundance of information, going back to the break-up of British North America during the Revolutionary War and continuing to the present day, that enables us to discern how these neighbors – "Children of a common mother," as declared by the inscription on the Peace Arch, at the border between Washington state and British Columbia – have viewed one another, why they have held these views, and what the consequences of these images of the other have been. These are the questions addressed by American historian Gordon T. Stewart in his important book, *The American Response to Canada since 1776* (Stewart 1992). Stewart's focus, in his own words, "is on policy thinking at the federal level," and thus his heavy reliance on State Department files on US–Canada relations and what they reveal about the images of Canada held by American decision-makers over the two centuries that he covers.

The ideas and images of decision-makers may not be identical to those of the general public. Indeed, they can sometimes be quite different. For example, Andrei Markovits is among those who have made the argument that until the beginning of the 20th century, anti-Americanism was much more prevalent and even virulent among European elites than among the mass publics of their respective countries (Markovits 2007; also Hollander 1995). In Canada too, the tendency toward anti-Americanism has been stronger among cultural and political elites than in the general population.[8] Thus, when we seek to understand the image that one country has of another, we need to be careful not to attribute a uniformity of views to an entire population. Not only may elite and mass views differ but there may be important variations between different segments of the general public or between different elites.

National images have both a cognitive and an affective component. The first involves beliefs about the attributes of a nation, including its economy, military capacity, geography, political system, cultural values and beliefs, history, and what might be described as its goals.[9] The second involves sentiment. It can involve something as simple as feeling more or less favorable toward a nation, approving or disapproving of its performance or behavior on the world stage or in relation to its neighbors, but also more nuanced judgments, such as whether a nation is trustworthy and a friend, ally, rival, or enemy. It may also involve assessments of whether a nation is similar to or different from one's own, and whether it is superior or inferior in some respects. Finally, there is also a valence aspect to sentiment: its intensity may be stronger or weaker. The cognitive and affective components of a national image are related. It is impossible to have a sentiment toward a nation without some cognitive basis on which this rests, even if this basis is flimsy and uninformed.

In the next two chapters, we will examine the images that Americans and Canadians have held of each other. This will be followed by an analysis of the role that these national images have played in shaping bilateral relations between these two neighbors. We will see that the asymmetrical relationship between the United States and Canada has resulted in a corresponding lopsidedness when it comes to the influence of national images on politics and policy. The national image of the United States held by Canadians and their leaders has often been an important determinant of policies, both foreign and domestic. When this has been the case, there has been an alignment between a significant part of elite opinion and that of the general public. From the American side, perceptions of Canada have rarely had an important impact on the country's bilateral dealings with its northern neighbor and have seldom affected domestic politics in the United States. When they have, however, this has been almost entirely due to some part of elite opinion. American public opinion has not been a factor affecting US–Canada relations since the early decades of the Republic.

Notes

1. This is not mere surmise. I was the researcher for Cellucci's published memoir of his time as the United States Ambassador to Canada, *Unquiet Diplomacy*. Over the course of that project, we had many conversations on this episode in US–Canada relations.
2. The four were the colonies of Newfoundland, Nova Scotia, Prince Edward Island, and Quebec. The fifth was the British colony of Bermuda.
3. A very early example of education and sophistication providing no immunity to rather crude and caricatured images of other peoples is provided by Jacques de Vitry in his account of the life of students at the University of Paris in the late 12th century. Among the scholars, these stereotypes were widely held: "The English were drunkards . . . the sons of France proud, effeminate and adorned like women . . . the Germans were furious and obscene at their feasts . . . the Sicilians, tyrannical and cruel," and so on (de Vitry, date unknown, but circa 1200: https://archive.org/details/libraryoriginal08thatgoog/page/n380/mode/2up?view=theater, p. 357).
4. The original goal of the VOA was to counter German and Japanese war propaganda. It quickly assumed the role of countering Soviet propaganda after World War II.
5. Sam Rohdie goes so far as to argue that:

    The love of the American cinema by Sartre and de Beauvoir was essentially aesthetic and philosophical rather than political except perhaps for its social bias, its popularity and populism. It is tempting to imagine, after Simone de Beauvoir's remarks referring to her and Sartre at a screening in 1931, that it was cinema that gave birth to Sartre's philosophy.

    (Rohdie, undated)

6. Laurier's optimistic projection was perhaps understandable in view of the spike in immigration that Canada experienced during the early years of the 20th century. Just under three million immigrants arrived in the country in the years from 1901 through 1914. The entire population of Canada in 1914 was just under eight million persons.
7. Part of the explanation for this failure on the part of the Canadian government surely lies with Canada's federal constitution, which assigns primary responsibility for education and many cultural matters to the provinces. However, federalism did not stop the US government from taking an active and aggressive role in projecting that country's image abroad after World War II.
8. This tendency may appear, on the face of it, rather surprising, given that for decades, Canadian cultural and intellectual elites, particularly those on the left, have been avid readers of such progressive American periodicals and newspapers as *The Atlantic*, *Harper's*, *The New Yorker*, *The New York Review of Books*, and *The New York Times*. On the other hand, the interpretations of America found in these media sources tend to be critical of much of American politics and policy, reinforcing the anti-American predispositions of nationalist elites in English Canada.
9. Nations, as such, do not have goals. This does not stop people from ascribing goals to a nation, as Canadians often have, believing that "America" has aimed to annex Canada in some manner.

2
AMERICA
A Canadian Obsession

Introduction

In 2002, between the terrorist attacks of September 11, 2001, and the invasion of Iraq in 2003, the French intellectual Jean François Revel published a book entitled, *L'Obsession anti-américaine* (Revel 2002). It was a moment in modern history when, not for the first time, a wave of anti-American sentiment was gaining strength across much of the world, including France. In his book, Revel argues that this was not surprising. Anti-Americanism in France ranges across the ideological spectrum and has a history that goes back more than two centuries. With the rise of the United States' global preeminence in the mid-twentieth century, French anti-Americanism became an obsession. French historian Philippe Roger, whose book, *L'Ennemi américain: Généologie de l'anti-américainisme français* (Roger 2002), was published that same year as Revel's, agreed. "Anti-Americanism," he declares, "is a fundamental given in the cultural and political life of France."

A reader of either of these books is likely to conclude that among America's allies, none has been as vigorously and persistently anti-American, or for as long, as the French. Without taking anything away from French anti-Americanism, Canadians might have something to say about such a claim. In important ways, Canadians are the original anti-Americans. Although Canadians' animus toward the United States has not assumed the virulent forms witnessed in some other parts of the world, any explanation of their country's historical development, its politics, and its culture, is unthinkable without acknowledging the enormous and persistent influence of their southern neighbor. This influence has not always been welcomed.

The birth of Canada, one might say, was a result of the successful independence of the 13 British colonies that became the United States. As the American sociologist, Seymour Martin Lipset, writes, "Americans do not know but Canadians

DOI: 10.4324/9781032675220-2

cannot forget that two nations, not one, came out of the American Revolution" (Lipset 1990, 1). The two nations, he argues, were the United States, the country of the successful revolution against British colonial rule, and what would become Canada, the British North American colonies to the north and northwest of the Thirteen Colonies, that remained loyal to Britain. Thus was set in motion the independent, but inextricably linked trajectories of two countries that, as the inscription on the American side of the Peace Arch at the border of British Columbia and Washington state reads, are "Children of a Common Mother."

Lipset goes on to argue that Canadians "are the world's oldest and most continuing anti-Americans." And so it might seem incongruous to find, on the Canadian side of the Peace Arch, the inscription, "Brethren Dwelling together in Unity." In order to reconcile what, on the face of it, appear to be two quite different messages about relations between the United States and Canada, it is necessary to consider how they have viewed one another since the moment of their historic separation. The Canadian view of America and Americans is the subject of this chapter.

Early Perceptions: Anti-American Elites and an Unconvinced Public

Those who have written Canadian history, or at least those versions that have been written by English Canadians,[1] have favored what I will call the semi-official nationalist narrative of what this separation signified and how it has mattered over the centuries. One of the cherished beliefs of this narrative – as expressed over the years through the state-owned Canadian Broadcasting Corporation (CBC) and school textbooks, among other purveyors of ideas about Canada–US differences – is that those who founded what would become Canada were significantly different from those who founded the United States. This is sometimes referred to as the Loyalist Myth, a reference to those who were on the losing side of the American War of Independence, many of whom subsequently migrated north (Fellows 1971). The population of what remained of British North America was, undeniably, different in some obvious ways. The colony of Quebec, formerly la Nouvelle France until its transfer to Britain in 1763, was overwhelmingly French-speaking and Catholic. But in the case of the English-speaking population of British North America after the War of Independence, they spoke the same language as Americans and were not significantly different in ethnic, religious, or socio-economic terms.

Nevertheless, the semi-official narrative insists that there were important cultural differences between them and that among these was the rejection by the English-speaking founders of Canada of what they saw as a foreign and undesirable value system. In other words, this narrative maintains that these early Canadians and *canadiens* perceived the fledgling United States and Americans in a negative light and, moreover, that this hostile perception led them to create and defend a society and institutions that were self-consciously and by design not American.

There is an element of truth in the semi-official narrative of Canadian history. But it exaggerates both the extent of the differences that separated Canadians and Americans culturally and the degree to which general opinion among Canadians and *canadiens* – as distinct from influential elements of elite opinion – embraced a negative image of America and Americans. There is plenty of evidence in the historical record that challenges this narrative.

Much of this evidence is examined by historian Reginald Stuart in his book, *Dispersed Relations: Americans and Canadians in Upper North America* (Stuart 2007). He argues that the relationship between Canada and the United States, both historically and in more recent times, has been shaped principally by transnational economic, social, and cultural factors – what Stuart calls "inescapable fundamental forces" – that governments have reacted to and often tried to manage, but with limited success. The semi-official history of this bilateral relationship emphasizes the jurisdictional and cultural border separating the two countries, and the role played by governments in maintaining this boundary and managing the relationship. But this border, Stuart argues, has never existed when it comes to the forces that do most to shape the bilateral relationship. "If you think Canadian-American relations are all about Ottawa and Washington," he says, "you've missed 98 percent of what's going on" (Stuart 2012).

Stuart's emphasis on the forces flowing below the pronouncements of governments and the perspectives of political elites – pronouncements and perspectives that history has tended to privilege – suggests that we should be wary of the argument that Canadians have always been concerned to protect their society and its political system from American influences. In the case of French Canadians, P.B. Waite suggests that popular sentiment among *les habitants* at the time of the American Revolution was probably in favor of joining the upstart colonies in their revolution against British rule (Waite 1965, 56–57). The idea that the French-speaking Catholic population of Quebec sought refuge behind the British crown from the threatening tide of liberalism to the south is also questioned by political scientist Denis Monière (Monière 1981). Like Waite, Monière argues that this perception of America certainly existed among members of the French-Canadian clergy, pleased as they were with the protections granted to them under the Quebec Act of 1774. But it was not shared by the *peuple* on whose behalf they claimed to speak.

The belief that rejection of American values and institutions was strong and widespread is central to the story of English Canada's origins, but here too the semi-official narrative projects onto history a large dose of contentious interpretation and dubious claims. An estimated 30,000–60,000 Loyalists emigrated north from the Thirteen Colonies after the War of Independence, adding to the pre-existing Anglophone population of about 15,000 in the British North American colonies. Speaking of those who settled in what would become Ontario, Kenneth McRae writes, "The Upper Canada Loyalists became simply a phase in the unrolling of the North American frontier, living with [those already there] and indistinguishable from them in any social sense" (McRae 1964, 236).

In the colony of New Brunswick, the immigrants from the newly independent United States far outnumbered the pre-war population, and about 90 percent of them were American-born. This helps to explain what P.B. Waite describes as the pro-American sympathies of the New Brunswick population before the Confederation. "New Brunswick had a distinctly American orientation both in political thought and practice," Waite remarks, "and its relations with Great Britain resembled those of more distinct colonies" (Waite 1962, 25). Nonetheless, some had a rather critical view of American society. Edward Winslow, a New Brunswick Loyalist, spoke for them when he said, "By heaven, we will be the envy of the American states" (quoted in Waite 1962, 14). Winslow was no admirer of the republic being created to the south. Nevertheless, it is easy to detect in his prediction that Americans would come to envy their northern neighbors the sort of pride born of insecurity that has so often characterized Canadian anti-Americanism.

Voices such as Winslow's – those of colonial elites in British North America – are generally taken to be representative of Canadian public opinion during the formative pre-Confederation decades of the Canada–US relationship. Indeed, S.F. Wise, in his study of colonial attitudes toward the United States between the War of 1812 and Canadian Confederation in 1867, begins with this premise: "[I]t is doubtful that the views of the inarticulate majority of Canadians were much different from those of their political spokesmen" (Wise 1967, 16–17). This is, of course, a premise whose validity is by no means obvious. The 19th-century colonial views of America and of the American political system that Wise examines are exclusively those of the Tory governing elites in British North America, views that could be summed up as follows. The American democracy was anarchic, divisive, and unnatural in its rejection of the proper order of things. That proper order involved was one in which society and the state would be presided over by "a Sovereign who loves and is the Father of his People" (Parker 1911, quoted in Wisc, 24).

Waite reminds us that what we think we know about Canadian public opinion toward the United States during the 19th century is based mainly on what was written in colonial newspapers and said in the legislatures. It is not clear, he argues, that these same views were held by the public on whose behalf these opinion-leaders claimed to speak (Waite 1962, 14). Goldwin Smith, the prominent Oxford historian who lived the last four decades of his life in Toronto (1872–1910), agreed they were not. "Of the antipathy to Americans sedulously kept up within select circles and in certain interests, there is absolutely none among the Canadian people at large," he writes. "It would be strange if there were any, considering that half of them have brothers, sons, or cousins on the American side of the Line" (Smith 1891, 270).

Indeed, there is abundant evidence showing that not only did much of the rank-and-file population not share the anti-American prejudices of the colonial elites but they also embraced values and behaved in ways virtually identical to those of the other side of the border. Susanna Moodie's well-known book, *Roughing It in the Bush* (1852), was by no means a systematic analysis of the values and behavior of the population of Upper Canada, nor is it free of the class biases that she brought with her from England. But it is full of careful and astute observations of those she encountered during what she came to think of as a regrettable sojourn in the New World. At every turn, she was struck and irritated by the egalitarian manners of those who, as an educated woman raised in a genteel and well-off family, and who was married to a former British military officer with a certain standing back home, she found obnoxious. Moodie believed that life in the frontier circumstances of Upper Canada, and in British North America more generally, was infected by the regrettable republican outlook and vulgarity that characterized the United States. There is little in her account of life and society in the colonies to suggest that she found the prevailing values to be different from those south of the border.[2]

Inference about the values of the colonial populace and, in particular, their views of the United States may perhaps be reasonably drawn from patterns of emigration. If the people of the Canadian colonies were as attached to living under the British crown and as anti-American as were most of those in their elites during the pre-Confederation era, then it seems probable that they would have been content to stay in Canada. Most did, but very large numbers of them did not. Instead, they left for the United States in numbers that far exceeded those who emigrated north. This was true among the Canadian-born and those who immigrated to Canada from Europe and then moved on to the United States. Moreover, this was happening during the very years when the colonial governments, particularly that of Upper Canada, were so concerned to tip the balance of the population toward those from the British Isles.[3] In 1849, the scale and persistence of this out-migration to the United States prompted study by a legislative committee of the United Canadas in what historical demographer Bruno Ramirez notes would be a series of such investigations over the years (Ramirez 2001, 53). Lest it be thought that these were mainly French Canadians leaving the farms of Quebec during the mid- and late 19th century for employment in the New England region of the United States – a story that is well known – Ramirez notes that "for every French-Canadian who immigrated to the United States, two Anglo-Canadians did likewise" (Ramirez, 59).

It might be objected that this emigration, among both French and English Canadians, was economically motivated, and, of course, this is true. But this simply confirms Reginald Stuart's insistence on "inescapable fundamental forces" as the drivers of movement back and forth across an international border that, until the 20th century, was not much more than a surveyor's line. The fine talk from Canada's governing classes, both French- and English-speaking, about the superiority of their country's institutions and values to those of the United States appears to have played little part in the decisions of average people as to whether they should stay or go.

More precisely, however, how did they imagine America, the country in which they decided to relocate? For many, the answer appears to have been as a place that promised more prosperity than was on offer in Canada. While it is certainly true that some of those who left Canada for the United States experienced hardship and disappointment, and some returned, the evidence suggests that this was not the experience of most and, indeed, many of those who emigrated were followed by family members. Speaking of the hundreds of thousands of French Canadians who emigrated beginning around the mid-19th century, Damien-Claude Bélanger writes,

> Upon their return to Quebec, whether temporary or permanent, emigrants frequently painted an idyllic vision of New England factory life and encouraged many of their relatives or neighbours to try their luck aux États . . . . The emigrant often became the symbol of success, stimulating others to follow his path to industrial New England.
>
> *(Bélanger 2000)*

The image of the United States as a land of far greater opportunity and prosperity than existed for many in Quebec is lyrically expressed in *Maria Chapdelaine*, the classic novel of *le Québec d'autrefois*. Lorenzo Suprenant, who left his native Quebec to work in a Massachusetts mill, returns to persuade Maria to marry him and leave her native country for the United States.

> This . . . is no place for you, Maria. The country is too rough, the work too hard; barely earning one's bread is killing toil. In a factory over there, clever and strong as you are, soon you would be in the way of making nearly as much as I do; but no need of that if you were my wife. I earn enough for both of us, and we should have every comfort: good clothes to wear, a pretty flat in a brick house with gas and hot water, and all sorts of contrivances you never heard of to save you labour and worry every moment of the day. And don't let the idea enter your head that all the people are English. I know many Canadian families who work as I do or even keep shops. And there is a splendid church with a Canadian priest as curé – Mr. Tremblay from St. Hyacinthe. You would never be lonesome.
>
> *(Hémon 1921)*

Ultimately, Maria rejects Lorenzo's entreaties and the image of the United States that he offered. But vast numbers of her compatriots did not.

As for English Canadians who emigrated to the United States, it is highly probable that most of their stories were broadly similar. "But it was the streets of gold in the American republic," writes Alan Brookes, "which proved to be the strongest and, in many cases, not-too-distant magnets [for Canadian emigrants]" (Brookes 1976, 39). In his study of out-migration from the Canadian maritime provinces between 1860 and 1900, Brookes calculates that roughly three-quarters of the very large number of those who left the Maritimes emigrated to the United States rather than to other parts of Canada (Brookes, 39–40). If the anti-Americanism and preference for British institutions characteristic of so many of their leaders had existed at the level of the general public, one might have expected that a much greater percentage would have been reluctant to relocate and live under the flag of the American republic.

In fact, however, the pull of familiar social and political institutions seems to have weighed rather lightly in the balance for most average citizens, compared to that of economic considerations. In their study of British immigrants to Canada between 1870 and 1910, Green and his colleagues conclude that "there is no need to assume that UK emigrants who chose to live in Canada [instead of leaving for the United States] were deeply committed to British traditions and the British empire" (Green 2002, 694). Most of the UK emigrants to Canada during this period "had occupational outcomes similar to those of their peers in the US, and probably only modestly lower annual earnings" (Green, 694), suggesting that economic forces explained whether one stayed or left.

Once in the United States, English-speaking Canadians experienced almost nothing in the way of the ethnic discrimination that faced some immigrant groups. Indeed, they usually were not even noticed, blending into their new home in ways that made them essentially indistinguishable from those already there. Brookes notes that the only instance of what he calls a "cohesive Maritime social identity" in Boston during the period 1860–1900, when large numbers of Maritimers emigrated to this city, was a newspaper for expats called the *American Canadian*. It disbanded after two years of publication, apparently unable to interest Maritimers in the news from "home," and despite the fact that its years of operation, 1874–76, were during the high point of Maritime emigration to the United States and to the city of Boston (Green, 49).

The impressive scale of emigration from Canada to the United States in the late 19th century has been well documented (Edmonston 2016, Table A1, 112; see also Jackson 1923). At a minimum, it suggests that the anti-Americanism of much of Canada's elites, both French- and English-speaking, was not shared by the general population. Immigration would surpass emigration by a wide margin during the first three decades of the 20th century – particularly during the economic boom that coincided with the rapid settlement of the Canadian West and what has been called the "Wheat Boom," but emigration, the vast majority of which was to the United States, remained high. Revealingly, perhaps, native-born Canadians accounted for the vast majority of this movement from Canada to the United States (Edmonston, Table A2, 116). As Goldwin Smith famously said, if the United States was not annexing Canada, it was certainly annexing Canadians (Smith, 233).

Despite the best efforts of the colonial elites, it simply is inaccurate to say that the population of the British North American colonies was anti-American. Brebner describes the people of Nova Scotia in the 1850s as "neutral Yankees" (Brebner 1937), noting that they consisted largely of transplanted New Englanders. Indeed, in some quarters, there was genuine envy of America and Americans. Joseph Howe, a leading Nova Scotia politician and one of the Fathers of Confederation, expressed these sentiments in a speech he made in 1854. Reminiscing about a dinner he had been invited to with John Quincy Adams and some of America's other leading men, he confessed that he envied their "boundless field" of ambition and lamented the "state of pupilage that men like himself in Canada experienced compared to their American cousins" (quoted in Waite 1962, 14).

Envy may lead to imitation or rejection. The envy that Howe felt was certainly shared by many of his Canadian contemporaries. Many of them dealt with it by emphasizing the differences between the values and institutions of the two societies and insisting on the superiority of Canada's. "It was in fact the young, energetic, ambitious journalists," says P.B. Waite, "who expressed most vividly the frustration with colonial status . . . [S]ituated between Great Britain and the United States, [these opinion leaders] were incessantly tantalized by the power and renown of others" (Waite 1962, 14).

The image of the United States that was propagated by the "ambitious journalists" that Waite speaks of and that was shared by most members of the political classes in the British North American colonies by the time of Confederation was decidedly negative. It consisted of three main elements: a distrust of the North of the United States, whose large standing army after the Civil War and what were believed to be its continental territorial ambitions were seen as threats to Canada; skepticism about the principles and institutions of the American constitution, including the federal system of government; and a disdain for American political practices, which colonial leaders in Canada tended to see as vulgar and disorderly.

The first element in this proto-nationalist image of the United States was well expressed by Thomas D'Arcy McGee in a speech during the Confederation debates at Quebec City. "[The Americans] coveted Florida, and seized it," McGee warned, "they coveted Louisiana, and purchased it; they coveted Texas, and stole it. . . . The acquisition of Canada was the first ambition of the American [Republic] and never ceased to be so" (quoted in Waite 1962, 29). McGee was one of many in the colonies who argued for Canadian Confederation chiefly on the grounds that this was necessary to preclude what would otherwise be the inevitable and irresistible northern expansion of the United States.

The second element of this negative image of America focused on what were argued to be the flaws in the republic's system of government. "The [U.S.] Constitution was a document of mutual suspicion," wrote the Halifax Morning Chronicle in 1864, "State distrusted State, individually and collectively the States distrusted the central government. . . . The Federation was a loosely bound mass of incongruity from the beginning that neither courage nor power could rebind" (quoted in Waite 1962, 33). Rhetorical broadsides against the American Constitution were commonplace, and almost no one among Canadian opinion-leaders argued that there was much in the US system of government that should be emulated. But as influential a figure as John A. Macdonald, Canada's first prime minister, took a more measured view of the American constitutional experience. In a speech given in Halifax on September 4, 1864, Macdonald argued against the tendency of many of his fellow colonial leaders to dismiss the American system of government as a dismal failure:

> I consider [the U.S. Constitution] a marvellous exhibition of human wisdom. It was as perfect as human wisdom could make it, and under it the American States greatly prospered until very recently; but being the work of men it had its defects, and it is for us to take advantage by experience, and endeavour to see if we cannot arrive by careful study at such a plan as will avoid the mistakes of our neighbors....
>
> The dangers that have risen from [their] system we will avoid if we can agree upon forming a strong central government – a great Central Legislature – a constitution for a Union which will have all the rights of sovereignty except those that are given to the local governments. Then we shall have taken a great step in advance of the American Republic.

Finally, the third element of the proto-nationalist image of America was that it was a sort of chaotic mobocracy. "[American legislatures are filled with] demagogues, prizefighters, and other specimens of the genus vagabond," said the Barrie Northern Advance, "who can handle a bowie knife much better than a pen" (quoted in Waite 1962, 13). American politics was, of course, colorful and full of characters who were far from possessing the gravitas and distinguished bearing of generations of New England Brahmins like the Adam family, Daniel Webster, and Henry Cabot Lodge. Still, it is hard not to detect in such a sweeping condemnation of the American law-making class a rather undemocratic mistrust of the people's judgment and a preference for keeping the general population at a safe distance from the levers of power.

Another and more enduring part of the explanation for the anti-American views that predominated among Canada's colonial elites is offered by S.F. Wise. "[I]t was essential," he writes,

> for Canadians not to believe in the United States and to assume that the country they lived in was not a kind of subarctic, second-best America, but rather a genuine alternative to this revolution-born democracy, and organized upon principles and for purposes quite different from it.
>
> *(Wise 1967, 22)*

Psychological need, Wise argues, reinforced the conservative ideology and anti-Americanism of these elites. Indeed, much of what has been said and written about Canadian politics and identity over the years has its roots in this psychological need to both distinguish Canada from the United States and justify its separateness through a narrative of superiority. Twentieth-century ideas about Canada as a place where "freedom wears a crown" and as the "peaceable kingdom," in which peace, order, and good government were preferred over "by the people, for the people and of the people," can be traced back to these early criticisms of what were seen as inferior American political practices and values.[4]

The Rebellions of 1837–38: Rejection of the American Model?

Against all this evidence of a much greater anti-Americanism among the colonial elites than characterized the general public, some Canadian historians and opinion-leaders point to the failed rebellions of 1837 (Lower Canada) and 1838 (Upper Canada) as proof that there was, in fact, little popular support for American political values and institutions. It is true that the leaders of these rebellions appear to have vastly overestimated popular support for their cause. Newspaper publisher William Lyon Mackenzie, the leader of the rebellion in Upper Canada, was convinced that average people, most of whom were farmers, would be quick to rise up in support of rebellion. In a handbill that he had distributed just before the rebellion broke out, and in words that echo sentiments in the American Declaration of Independence, Mackenzie wrote:

> The law says we shall not be taxed without our consent by the voices of the men of our choice, but a wicked and tyrannical government has trampled upon that law....
>
> Canadians! Do you love freedom? ... Do you hate oppression? ... Do you wish perpetual peace, and a government founded upon the eternal heaven-born principle of the Lord Jesus Christ – a government bound to enforce the law to do to each other as you would be done by? ... Then buckle on your armour, and put down the villains who oppress and enslave our country.... One short hour will deliver our country from the oppressor; and freedom in religion, peace and tranquility, equal laws and an improved country will be the prize....
>
> I could never enumerate all the blessings attendant on independence [from British rule][1]
>
> *(quoted in Waite 1965, 106)*

Indeed, Mackenzie often borrowed from the liberal and republican language of the American Revolution, printing Patrick Henry's famous oration, "Give me Liberty or Give me Death" in his newspaper in 1837 and often including references to the Declaration of Independence in his editorials (MacKay 1937). The "Constitution for the State of Upper Canada," that he signed (if he did not actually participate in its writing) in November of 1837, was self-consciously modeled on the American 1776 Declaration:

> Government is founded on the authority, and is instituted for the benefit, of a people; when, therefore, any Government long and systematically ceases to answer the great ends of its foundation, the people have a natural right given them by their Creator to seek after and establish such institutions as will yield the greatest quantity of happiness to the greatest number.
>
> *(quoted in MacKay 1937, 17)*

Mackenzie's counterpart and leader of the rebellion in Lower Canada, Louis-Joseph Papineau, was also an admirer of American political values and institutions. Indeed, after the failure of the rebellion that he led and during his exile for several years in the United States, he became a staunch advocate of the annexation of Canada and the United States. But his admiration and his republicanism were filtered through his French Canadian nationalism. As Robert MacKay writes,

> It was by following the example of the Americans, [Papineau believed] that the French Canadians could recover their national genius and at the same time abolish those false elements with which they had been burdened by European traditions of aristocracy and monarchy.
> *(MacKay 1937, 12).*

But in neither case does it appear that a majority of the population in Upper Canada or the *peuple* of Lower Canada shared anything close to the fervor or philosophical justifications that Mackenzie and Papineau presented in support of rebellion against British colonial rule. That there was widespread dissatisfaction in both Upper and Lower Canada is without doubt. Much of this was almost certainly due to economic conditions, but in both Upper and Lower Canada, the experience of British rule without meaningful popular representation was a cause of discontent. In Lower Canada, the domination of elite positions by the English-speaking minority was an additional factor. In Upper Canada, the oligarchic rule of the "Family Compact," which controlled patronage and limited access to much of the arable land in the colony through what were known as the clergy and crown reserves, was also a major cause of resentment against the status quo. All of these grievances are, however, rather different from the pro-American views of those who led the rebellions in these two British colonies.

It is, however, a step too far to claim that the populations of Upper and Lower Canada were anti-American. Some were, just as some were pro-American. For most, however, the discontents mentioned above were of far greater import in their lives than whether American-style political institutions ought to be adopted in Canada. In the case of predominantly French-Canadian Lower Canada, Fernand Ouellet writes, "[W]hat value would there have been in independence and democracy for an illiterate population that had no middle class, was encircled by medieval institutions, and lived by an almost parasitical agriculture[al system]?" (Ouellet 1972, 21). The general population was not opposed to the republican institutions that excited Papineau's imagination. But they had no real knowledge of them, could not understand them, and were largely apolitical.

In the case of Upper Canada, and acknowledging the paucity of hard evidence, what one thought of American political institutions and values appear to have counted for little when it comes to explaining the willingness of some colonists to take up arms. But demography does. Colin Reed notes that most of the rebels were North American-born, many with roots in the United States, the British-born constituting perhaps one-third of rebels in the Toronto area and about one-fifth of those in the west of the colony. They were drawn overwhelmingly from protestant denominational groups other than the established Church of England. As to why they decided to take up arms against British rule, Read offers this explanation:

> [They had a] North American orientation which resented a distant power and a colonial system of government. . . . as well as the general reform perception that the world was ordered too much in the interests of the few, too little in the interests of the many.
>
> *(Read 1988, 18)*

In the end, the rebellions in Upper and Lower Canada tell us little about views of the United States among average people, as opposed to those who led the rebellions. The fact that they were put down rather quickly cannot be adduced as proof of the population's distaste for American political institutions and preference for life under the British crown. At the same time, the complexity and variety of reasons for rebellion – reasons that were not identical in the two colonies – should give pause to any who would draw the conclusion that these failed efforts to overturn colonial rule tell us very much about how the rebels who rallied behind Mackenzie and Papineau perceived their southern neighbor.

On the other hand, the fact that ideas about America were important elements in the arguments made by the rebellions' leaders is significant and would have enduring consequences. Pro-American sentiments in the Canadas, and particularly in Upper Canada, had existed for decades. But the rebellions represented the first time that such sentiments had achieved such prominence, being formulated into widely circulated manifestoes and succeeding in mobilizing armed resistance to colonial rule. It was a moment in time when the choice between the American model, or some adaptation of it, or even union with the United States, was posed as an alternative to the status quo of colonial rule. Even if the vast majority of colonists did not perceive the choice in these rather grand terms, the more radical of the reform leaders did. Throughout the subsequent history of Canada, the view that Canada and Canadians would be better off living under an American-style system of government, and perhaps even under a common flag, has been embraced by a minority. Indeed, as recently as 2001, one in five Canadians supported the idea of Canada being annexed by the United States (Leger 2001). Something short of annexation has been advocated in recent decades by some of Canada's prominent opinion-leaders, including business journalist and author Diane Francis (2013), former Canadian ambassador to the United States, Allan Gotlieb (2002), some of the country's most prominent economists, including Wendy Dobson (2002) and Steven Globerman (2008), as well as Canada's most media-cited think tank, the Fraser Institute. Nevertheless, when it comes to annexation with the United States, Canadians have been more likely to fear than to favor this option for their future.

Fears of Annexation

Fears among some in the British North American colonies that the United States coveted their territory may be dated from the War of 1812. As Reginald Horsman observes, statements by two American generals made early in that war were cited by the British peace negotiators at Ghent in 1814 as proof that the United States aimed to conquer British North America and annex the colonies (Horsman 1987, 2). This charge was rejected by the negotiators at the peace talks, and indeed there is no evidence that it was a direct cause of the war. That it might have been desired by some American politicians is another matter (Stanley 1983, 29). But their reasons for favoring annexation almost certainly had less to do with grand notions of Manifest Destiny than with fear of the British presence on their border and on the seas (see Chapter 3).

By the mid-19th century, the lessening of tensions between the United States and Britain, combined with support from some economic interests in both the United States and the British North American colonies, led to negotiations over trade reciprocity (Haynes 1892). The first such treaty was agreed in 1854 and continued until its abrogation by the American government in 1866.[5] The issue of reciprocity, or free trade as it would more commonly be called by the mid-20th century, served as a lightning rod for political division and polarized views of the United States even before Canadian Confederation in 1867 and continues to be a source of significant political division in Canada today. It is an issue that, for much of Canada's early history, was linked to fears of annexation by the United States.

The end of the Reciprocity Treaty of 1854 was immediately followed by fresh evidence that the real design of the United States was the annexation of the British colonies. In an 1865 speech given in Detroit, the American consul in Montreal made the following statement:

> We are ready to give you in Canada the most perfect reciprocity. We will give you complete free trade, but we ask you to come and share with us the responsibilities of our government.... I believe I express the general feeling of those who are the most friendly to the United States in Canada when I say it is not the policy of our government, or our policy, to continue this treaty, and I believe that in two years from the abrogation of the reciprocity treaty the people of Canada themselves will apply for admission to the United States.
>
> *(quoted in Lauck, 502)*

Such sentiments did not go unnoticed among the politicians and opinion-leaders of the colonies. Indeed, they reinforced an already existing predisposition among many of them to believe that the end goal of American policy was annexation. Although this had never been the official policy of any American administration, there was no shortage of prominent advocates of this policy in the 1860s, including President Lincoln's secretary of state, William Seward (see Smith 1891; Smith 1933, 6). There is little doubt that fear of annexation, particularly of the vast and sparsely populated western territories that were under the control of the Hudson's Bay Company, was one of the principal drivers of the movement for Confederation.

FIGURE 2.1 *A Pertinent Question.*

Mrs. Britannia, "Is it possible, my dear, that you have ever given your cousin Jonathan any encouragement?"
Miss Canada, "Encouragement! Certainly not, Mamma. I have told him we can never be united."

Image from J.W.A. Bengough, *A Caricature History of Canadian Politics. Toronto:* The Grip Printing & Publishing Co., 1886.

Fear of American annexation was not shared by all Canadians. Some of those who were active in the rebellions that took place in Upper and Lower Canada in 1837 and 1838, respectively, were not only admirers of American political institutions but favorable toward annexation. Throughout the remainder of that century there would be a minority within the Canadian population that saw eventual integration of Canada into the United States as both inevitable and desirable (Smith 1891; Bender 1883). Nevertheless, during an era when

Prime Minister John A. Macdonald could declare, "A British subject I was born – a British subject I will die," the prospect of annexation by the United States could be used to considerable political effect. These words of Macdonald's were spoken during the 1891 Canadian election, fought on the issue of reciprocity with the United States. This was not a cynical and disingenuous attempt on his part to stir up anti-Americanism and wrap himself in the flag of British patriotism. "Every American statesman covets Canada," Macdonald added, "The greed for its acquisition is still on the increase" (quoted in Marsh 2015).

This would turn out to be a mere, albeit important, prelude to the 1911 Canadian election in which the Reciprocity Agreement between Canada and the United States, approved by Congress in 1911, was the issue that overshadowed all others. Political cartoons published in Canadian newspapers before and during the campaign portrayed a rapacious and greedy Uncle Sam and the American trusts, the latter sometimes represented by an enormous pig at the trough, playing to fears of annexation. A decade after the 1911 Canadian election, economist Harold S. Paton wrote,

> it was strenuously urged [by opponents of reciprocity] that the opening of the trade gates on the frontier . . . would be the first step in American economic and eventual political domination in Canada. The bogey of annexation, supported by certain garbled utterances of Mr. Taft and the American press, was luridly projected on the near horizon. Canadian nationality and imperial loyalty were represented as directly at stake.
> *(Paton 1921, 579)*

MacKenzie and Dutil put it this way: "[I]n 1911, Canadians were inundated with a flood of rhetoric that was a mixture of patriotic bombast, nationalistic fear-mongering, jingoistic support for the Empire, and pure anti-Americanism" (MacKenzie 2011, 182).

The reciprocity issue and the passions that it inflamed demonstrate two key aspects of the Canadian image of the United States. One is that Canadians have never been of a single mind when it comes to their beliefs about either American intentions toward Canada or the consequences of greater integration with their southern neighbor. The other involves Canadian identity. From the initial refusal of the northernmost British colonies to join with the Thirteen Colonies in the enterprise of independence, the construction, affirmation, and defense of a Canadian sense of identity would be built on a foundation of beliefs about and sentiments toward the United States. To put it differently, albeit a bit simply, without an image of America, there is no self-image of Canada, at least in English-speaking Canada.

Ironically, only two years before the Canadian election of 1911, a treaty had been signed between the United States and Great Britain on Canada's behalf[6] that would soon come to be heralded by many Canadian political officials as a model of bilateral cooperation for the world. The International Boundary Waters Treaty (1909) involved shared sovereignty and consensus decision-making in water matters along the world's longest border. It was an early pillar of what Canadians would come to refer to in the post-World War II era as the "special relationship" between their country and the United States.

Canadian Ambivalence Toward America

By the early 20th century, the die was cast. The Canadian image of the United States was a mixture of admiration and wariness, but above all, ambivalence. To be more precise, this ambivalence was characteristic of the distribution of attitudes and beliefs about the United States and Americans across the Canadian population. Some persons held overwhelmingly negative attitudes, while others, a smaller share of the Canadian population, held consistently and strongly positive views. But ambivalence was also a characteristic of the images held by individual Canadians, a significant portion of whom held both negative and positive views of their southern neighbors.

The nature of this ambivalence is suggested by the findings of interviews and surveys carried out in the 1930s as part of the Carnegie series on Canadian–American relations and published in *Canada and Her Great Neighbor* (Angus and MacIver 1938). These surveys and interview panels were not national in scope. Rather, they focused on groups of teachers and students in various provinces, on community groups that, in the worlds of S.D. Clark, one of the collaborators on this study, "were thought to be representative and who were expected to be communicative" (Angus 1938, 383), and on groups consisting of persons who were considered to be opinion-leaders in their local communities or provinces (see Angus 1938, 405–406). Although by no means a nationally representative sample of public opinion, this pioneering effort to gauge the attitudes and beliefs of Canadians toward their country's "Great Neighbor" was the first systematic analysis of these views to rely on measurable data.

What it found was a picture of widespread ambivalence, captured in one researcher's observation that "few of those who were interviewed had well-organized, or even consistent, opinions about the United States" (Angus 1938, 383). One of the surveys administered for this project asked respondents about the ways in which each country was superior to the other. Canada was seen by most to be superior when it came to control of crime, law and justice, and government and politics, whereas the United States was thought by most to be superior in manufacturing and industry, transportation, and aviation, and also in terms of progressiveness, resourcefulness, and energy (Angus 1938, 371–372). These assessments were echoed in many of the interviews, the findings of which included not only widespread belief in the greater materialism, laxer morals, and greater corruption of the legal and justice systems in the United States but also greater energy, ambition, and willingness to innovate and take risks among Americans.

In short, the Carnegie study corroborated the existence of stereotypes that were evident from a perusal of such general interest magazines of politics, culture, and current affairs as *Maclean's* and *Saturday Night*, newspaper articles and editorials, political cartoons, and school textbooks, among the sources of information and images of the United States and Americans. Canada's foremost popular historian of his generation, Pierre Berton, describes a Canadian magazine cartoon that impressed him as a boy in the 1920s. It pictured, "Uncle Sam, looking more villainous than ever, down on his knees, holding a sack of bullion over his head, worshipping 'Strange Gods'" (Berton 1982, 57). Such images were common in the Canadian press. The popular belief among Canadians that Americans were more concerned with money and material possessions at the expense of other values – superior Canadian values! – was a staple of journalism in English-speaking Canada at a moment in time when the country's image of itself was still very much that of a member of the British Empire.

The stereotypes that prevailed in Canada were not particularly different from those found in many other countries at that moment in history, when America's economic ascendance was evident and growing, and its cultural influence was beginning to explode across the western world and, in the process, attract the worried attention of critics abroad. Georges Duhamel's *America the Menace* (1931), Simone de Beauvoir's *America, Day by Day* (1999), and Harold Laski's *The American Democracy* (1948) the misgivings of many prominent intellectuals this era about America's spreading cultural influence[7] (see Markovits 2007).

Leaving aside the accuracy of the stereotypes about America that were held prior to World War II by Canadians and other national populations, an important change had taken place in the sources that gave rise to and that helped perpetuate them. "The basis of the Canadian picture of the United States," Angus and MacIver write, "is to be found in the American press, the American motion pictures and American radio programs" (12). Prior to the 1930s, print media and personal experiences were the main sources of Canadian images of America. These continued to be influential, but with the rise of Hollywood, film quickly became the dominant source for Canadians' image of America.

It goes without saying that the American film industry's portrayal of life and values in the United States was influenced by commercial considerations. Twentieth Century Fox, Paramount, MGM, and the other major studios were not in the business of producing documentaries. Thus, the image of America that was projected onto screens in cinemas across the world, not just in Canada, was one that leaned heavily toward representations and stories expected to attract mass audiences and make money. In Canada, Hollywood's portrayal of vice, corruption, avarice, and materialism contributed to and reinforced the pre-existing tendency among many Canadians to see their own country as morally, culturally, and politically superior to the country whose stories they found so riveting (Angus and MacIver 1938).

Indeed, it may be true that Americans have long been more individualistic and materialistic than Canadians, although it is doubtful that the difference between the populations has ever been as significant as some have argued. But whether the reality was more nuanced than stark in the early twentieth century, the belief in this image was promoted in Canadian schools and the materials used in teaching about America. A study by Amy Von Heyking of textbooks used in Canada throughout the 20th century found that most characterizations of American values and behavior were negative. "In the early part of the twentieth century, there's a sense of moral superiority in our treatment, and it's coming from a conservative education elite," observes Von Heyking. "By the end of the century," she says, "there's the same sense of cultural and even moral superiority – we as Canadians understand the world – but it's now coming from a left education establishment" (Von Heyking 2006, 407).

We will return later in this chapter to the second part of Von Heyking's conclusion about the image of America taught in Canadian schools, including the country's universities. First, however, we need to focus on that moment in history when Canada was moving inexorably from the orbit of the British Empire into that of the ascendant American empire, when Canadians were becoming as mesmerized by the images produced by Hollywood as were their southern neighbors.

In a series of lectures given at Columbia University in 1933–34, Canada's foremost English-speaking journalist, John W. Dafoe, told his listeners that Canada's imports from the United States had been well over half of his country's total for over three decades and that Canada's trade with its southern neighbor accounted for over half of its entire trade with the rest of the world. Dafoe also observed that, according to numbers provided by the US census, one in seven persons born in Canada resided in the United States. He claimed to detect what he called a "great ebbing in the strength of this hereditary anti-American feeling" among Canadians, which Dafoe attributed to a growing confidence among Canadians regarding their independent nationhood. More specifically, the sense of being a junior partner in the British Empire and a British nation that happened to be located in North America was in decline. Dafoe did not hesitate to talk about a "North American civilization" (Dafoe 1935, 96) which, he added, was the joint possession of Canada and the United States.

Not everyone, however, was as sanguine as Dafoe about what he saw as the decline of a Canadian self-image linked to notions and symbols of Britishness or as relieved at the weakening of a "hereditary anti-American" feeling among Canadians. The ideas of the conservative educational elite that Von Heyking describes in her study of school materials were not so easily swept away. They were reinforced by those of other Canadian opinion-leaders for whom the British connection remained essential to their country's identity and in whose eyes American values and institutions were inferior and un-Canadian. "English-speaking Canadian thinkers," writes Daniel Horowitz, "continually negotiated between what they saw in the United States and what they derived from their British origins." He goes on to say, "For members of the Conservative Party, the United States represented individualism, the pursuit of happiness, a messianic commitment to transform the world, while Canada embraced the orderliness of an organic society and the national independence of a peaceful one" (Horowitz, 154). The only part that Horowitz gets wrong is his suggestion that these ideas were owned by members of Canada's Conservative Party. In fact, such ideas about America, and about the ways in which Canada was not a carbon copy of its neighbor, were widely held. Indeed, it was a Liberal government that established the government commission that led to the creation of the Canadian Broadcasting Corporation, and a Liberal government that created the National Film Board,[8] both of which were reactions to what was perceived to be American domination of Canadian culture. Moreover, it was a Liberal-appointed government commission that in its 1951 report spoke of an "American invasion" of Canada's popular culture and recommended measures for the "resistance of the absorption of Canada into the general cultural pattern of the United States" (Government of Canada 1951).

"Is Canada Being Americanized?" (Bretherton 1926). This was the question that already was posed in the title of a 1926 Mclean's magazine article, and that was a frequent subject of conversation in Canada even before the emergence of the American-dominated new media radio, film, and television, the bilateral integration that took place during World War II, close cooperation during the early years of the Cold War, and a massive increase in American direct investment in the Canada economy had occurred. The question was linked in large measure to culture. "If pro-British sentiment dies out," wrote British-American journalist Cyril Emmanuel Bretherton in 1926, "and the Canadian becomes simply a Canadian, economic considerations might easily pave the way to his becoming an American" (Bretherton 1926). In the same vein, William Baker writes, "For Canadians, the American menace between 1914 and 1965 was perhaps more social and cultural than political or economic" (Baker 1973, 70).

The American "menace," as Baker calls it, and as it was certainly viewed by most of English-Canada's cultural elite, would be joined by a resurgence of fears regarding American economic domination to a degree that had not been seen since the Reciprocity Election of 1911. But here we need to pause in order to recall that throughout Canadian history, going back to the pre-Confederation decades of the 19th century, there had always existed a gap between the perceptions of America held by Canadian elites and those held by the general public. It is common in discussing the rise of anti-American sentiment and of Canadian nationalism in the decades of the 1950s and 1960s to speak of the views of Canadians. This is, as was true during earlier periods in Canadian history, quite misleading. While there is little doubt that the general public became more aware of the issue of American influence on Canadian life in the post-World War II era and that polls showed that a significant share of the population agreed that this influence was too great, it is also true that they were primed to think about the issue of American influence by cultural and political elites for whom questions of American domination of Canadian airwaves, ownership of much of the Canadian economy, and limitations on Canada's political independence were passionate matters – matters of national survival, according to many – requiring state action.

We know what prominent Canadian journalists, politicians, and other opinion-leaders thought, but aside from poll results, we do not know nearly as much about the image of America held by the Canadian public during this era. But, as was true during earlier times, we can draw some inferences from their behavior. American magazines accounted for about 80 percent of the periodical market by the mid-1950s (Edwardson 2008, Chapter 3). At the same time, about half of all content shown on Canadian television was produced in the United States and roughly 80 percent of all viewing time in Canada's English-language market was devoted to American programs (Bumsted 1986, 405). Canadians did not appear particularly worried about this situation. A 1956 poll found that only about one in four agreed that the Canadian way of life was being influenced too much by the United States (cited in Granatstein and Bothwell 1991, 41).

Over the next couple of decades, the percentage of Canadians agreeing that the Canadian way of life was threatened by American influence would grow, to just over half in 1966 and to almost six in ten Canadians in 1974 (ibid.). At the same time, however, their behavior belied the responses they gave when prompted by pollsters' questions. Canadians' media consumption preferences remained overwhelmingly American, as indeed they are today. This incongruence between what is often taken to be a valid measure of Canadians' concern with American domination of their country, and behavior that suggests a preference for American popular culture, is frequently characterized as ambivalence. This was not, however, the conclusion reached by Canadian historian Frank Underhill. In his introduction to a volume on Canadian nationalism published in 1966, he asked, "[M]ay it not be that our ordinary rank-and-file Canadians have shown a deeper intuitive wisdom than most of their intellectual leaders?" Underhill doubted that the concerns of Canadian elites to build protective walls and barriers of various sorts around their country's culture and to protect those who produced it were shared by ordinary Canadians who, he observed, "have been adopting the American way of life" (Underhill 1966, xix). Nationalist elites pointed to the results of polls showing that Canadians were concerned with American influence. Underhill's response was that Canadians' behavior spoke more loudly and revealingly on this matter.

The "New" Canadian Nationalism

That Canadians believed their country's relationship to the United States was a subject worthy of public concern was hardly surprising. Between 1949 and 1972, no fewer than four royal commissions, a federal task force, and a special senate committee produced major and much discussed reports on aspects of American cultural and economic influence on Canada (Government of Canada 1951, 1955, 1957, 1960, 1972; Senate of Canada 1970). These influences were often discussed in the Canadian media, not infrequently in near-apocalyptic terms.

"It's the U.S. or Us!," declared Hugh MacLennan, one of English Canada's most celebrated writers during the post-World War II era.

> The Americanization of Canada – by which I mean the swamping of our national purpose by that of the United States and of our habits by a state of mind totally American – has been such a subconscious process on our part, and such an unmalicious one on theirs, that no reasonable man could call it a conquest.

It was, rather, a sort of seduction, he argued, in which Canadians were entirely complicit (MacLennan 1960). MacLennan's contemporary, Farley Mowat, went further. "Let's get roaring mad," he wrote in a rallying call to Canadian nationalists. The measured tones of the nationalist Massey Report are gone, replaced by a political militancy that would gain significant traction in Canada during the 1960s and 1970s:

> There is no need for me to list the formidable array of incontrovertible facts which prove conclusively that we are rapidly being engulfed by the United States. Despite the best efforts of the professional apologists and propagandists of radio, newspapers and magazines, these facts are undeniable. Even the most brotherly amongst us is uncomfortably aware of them. But there is a need for me to attempt the restoration of some honor to my caste, by speaking out against *this monstrous cult whose symbol is the benevolent image of our good neighbor to the south.*
>
> *(Mowat 1958, emphasis added)*

Magazine articles, newspaper op-eds, and television and radio interviews purveying the new Canadian nationalism were common during this era. What was "new" about the nationalism expressed by MacLennan, Mowat, and almost all of the major opinion-leaders of this era was the strident and often aggressive tone, as well as the insistence on the necessity of measures guaranteed to produce serious strain in the Canada–US relationship (Hutchison 1959; Lower 1958; Newman 1956).

There was some pushback, from such figures as novelist Morley Callaghan 1958), journalist Robert Fulford, and prominent radio and television broadcaster Gordon Sinclair. Indeed, Sinclair's 1973 radio editorial, "The Americans," would become iconic in the United States and was even mentioned gratefully by President Reagan during his 1981 visit to Canada. Defense and admiration of America was, however, very much against the tide of the era and was noticeable on that account. The prevailing spirit of the age was that American influence had become too great and that, on the whole, its effects were negative. This, as we have seen, was already the essential plank in the proto-Canadian nationalism that emerged during the colonial era, embraced by much of the English-speaking elites, though not nearly as enthusiastically by the general population. What was new about the Canadian nationalism that emerged during the 1950s and 1960s was the idea that the United States represented a comprehensive and existential threat to Canadian values and institutions, and even to Canadian political sovereignty.

This new turn in Canadian nationalism found its most prominent voice in the writings of the philosopher and descendant of Loyalists, George Grant. His book, *Lament for a Nation: The Defeat of Canadian Nationalism* (1970), argued that the possibility of an independent Canada that is not dominated in all important respects by the agents of American power, including American corporations, cultural industries, and US government policies, had become impossible. The book became must reading for Canadian nationalists across the ideological spectrum and Grant became synonymous among Canadian opinion-leaders with resistance to what he described as the "technological bulldozer of the American empire."

Lament for a Nation was not specifically about America's role and influence in the world, although it was situated within an interpretation of that influence that by this point was highly critical and not particularly original. In *Technology and Empire*, published a few years later, Grant elaborated on the argument already made in his lament for what he deemed to be the end of the possibility of genuine Canadian independence from the United States. America was, he argued, merely the chief embodiment and the principal motor of

> a universally-administered, technology-driven, homogenous society . . . this future society would necessarily be a tyranny [although it would wear a mask], one that would unhinge peoples the world over from all national customs and traditions, their character and lives instead would be determined by the needs of unbridled change and technological advance.
>
> *(Bickerton 2006, 37)*

Corporate power wedded to an American notion of progress would ensure this bleak outcome.

Sixty years after the publication of *Lament for a Nation*, the scope and duration of its influence may be gleaned from the fact that it remains the single most recognizable title, by far, from an era that generated a profusion of nationalist books. They included such evocative titles as *Silent Surrender*, *Close the 49th Parallel*, *Independence: The Canadian Challenge*, *The New Romans: Candid Canadian Opinions of the United States*, and *(Canada) Ltd.: The Political Economy of Dependency*. These years also saw the creation of the Committee for an Independent Canada (1971), under the leadership of nationalist icon and former Liberal finance minister Walter Gordon. Grant was the philosopher of the new Canadian nationalism. But it was Gordon, with his roots in the Toronto business world and deep ties to the Liberal Party, who more than anyone ensured that the new nationalism would enter the mainstream of Canadian politics. There it would remain until the 1980s (Azzi 1999).

As was true of the tide of anti-Americanism that gained strength throughout western democracies in the 1960s and 1970s, the new Canadian nationalism was strongly influenced by the global role that the United States had assumed during and after World War II. Opposition to American involvement in Vietnam fueled increasing doubts about American global leadership among many western populations during the Cold War (Isernia 2007). The idea that the United States was part of the problem of global instability and conflict, rather than a necessary part of its solution – an idea that in the two decades immediately after World War II was mainly limited to the fringes of the intellectual and political left in western societies – became standard fare among those on the left and, in some societies such as France, was widely accepted across the ideological spectrum.

Vietnam was only part of the story behind what might be described as the declining standing of the United States in the eyes of many of its allies. As the politics of assassination, violent racial conflict, and political corruption plagued the domestic scene, the American empire appeared to many to be rotten, malevolent, and predatory. "The new anti-Americanism," declared Canadian journalist Robert Fulford in 1970, "begins with the proposition that the United States is a colossal empire and a corrupt one, and that its imperial designs are forcing its corrupt nature on us" (Fulford 1970, 12). This was certainly the view among English Canada's left nationalists who came to dominate political science, sociology, media studies, and history departments in Canadian universities (Brooks and Gagnon 1988, Chapter 5). It was also expressed through the country's social democratic party, the New Democratic Party, and embraced by many in the left-leaning, more nationalist wing of the Liberal Party. The image of the United States as a militaristic bully with no serious claim to the moral high ground over the Soviet Union, its Cold War rival, was embraced by many if not most members of the country's cultural elites and resonated with a significant share of the general public (Granatstein 1996). Indeed the Liberal prime minister of Canada for most of this period, Pierre Trudeau, was himself more than dubious about the role of America in the world, and at one point appeared to favor Canadian withdrawal from NATO (Kelly 2017). There is no evidence in his published memoirs that Trudeau ever saw the United States as less of a threat to world peace and stability than the Soviet Union.

Thus, an important and distinguishing aspect of the new Canadian nationalism that gained strength in the 1960s and 1970s was a strong disposition among Canadian elites, though weaker in the general population, to be critical of America's motives and consequences on the world stage (Sigler and Goresky 1974). This disposition was nurtured, to an important degree, by Canada's insecure identity in the shadow of its rather overwhelming neighbor. "When we look at Americans," said Canadian Ambassador to the United States, Allan Gotlieb, "we often do so to seek reassurance about our image of ourselves" (Gotlieb 1987). Canadian characterizations of their country as a "peacekeeper," "honest broker," "middle power," and "moral superpower" – this latter self-description was regularly used by some Canadian government officials in the 1990s – have been formulated alongside a much less flattering image of America's role in the world.

The new Canadian nationalism arose at the same time as the idea that Canada had a "special relationship" with the United States. When the actual term began to be used by Canadian opinion-leaders is not entirely clear. By the 1960s, however, and in response to the Canadian government's successful request for exemptions from American trade laws intended to deal with that country's balance of payments deficits, it was a familiar part of the Canadian conversation on the country's relationship with the United States. "Special," in this case, had a precise meaning. It signified that Canada would receive different and favorable treatment that was not likely to be extended to America's other economic partners. Since then and down to the present day, the term acts as a sort of benchmark and, for some, a gold standard when it comes to the assessment of the state of this bilateral relationship. Other Canadians disagree and view the idea of the special relationship as indicative of a sort of vassalage that their country should reject.

Multiculturalism as a Marker of Difference (and Superiority!)

In 1971, Canadian Prime Minister Pierre Trudeau announced that multiculturalism was the official policy of the government of Canada. This would prove to be an important development in the Canadian self-image and a new marker of difference from their neighbors to the south. The British-ness of Canada's identity – in English Canada, at least – served to distinguish the country from the United States into the early 20th century. As Canada moved from the orbit of its mother country (it fact its second mother country, the first being France) and into that of the world's ascendant power, the United States, this generated a nationalist response that attempted to create and articulate an identity that did not rely on Canada's British past. This identity construction enterprise was given a major boost when, for a combination of reasons that had almost nothing to do with a conscious desire to distinguish Canada's values and identity from those of the United States (Wayland 1997, 47), Canada adopted an official policy of multiculturalism in 1971. Before long, the idea took hold that Canadian multiculturalism represented something important about the "soul" of the country, distinguishing its brand of pluralism from the American model of *e pluribus unum*. Multiculturalism was enlisted in the very old practice of developing and nurturing a narrative of distinctiveness from the United States.

In fact, even before the word multiculturalism achieved widespread familiarity in the Canadian political conversation, the metaphor of Canada as a *mosaic*, contrasted to the American *melting pot*, was common and used in very much the same way that multiculturalism has been used for the past several decades. Ironically, it appears that the first recorded use of the mosaic metaphor in its application to Canada was from the pen of an American travel writer by the name of Victoria Hayward. In her 1922 book, *Romantic Canada*, she refers to Asian and Indigenous communities as part of the Canadian mosaic. *Our Canadian Mosaic* was the title of a book published four years later by Kate Foster for the Young Women's Christian Association. But it was in the 1930s that the term achieved widespread popularity and began to be contrasted to the American melting pot, through the writings of John Murray Gibbon, including his 1938 book, *Canadian Mosaic: The Making of a Northern Nation*. Indeed, the political usefulness of this contrast between the Canadian mosaic and the American melting pot seems to have been recognized by Governor-General John Buchan (1935–40) who, in Peter Henshaw's words, "encouraged Canadians to make multiculturalism a defining feature of Canadian identity and nationalism"[9] (Henshaw 2007, 191).

Since the 1970s, Canadian schoolchildren have learned that the key characteristic of Canadian culture and society and the cornerstone of the modern Canadian identity is tolerance of, openness toward, and the preservation of the ancestral cultures that immigrant groups have brought to Canada. In teaching this multicultural ethos, Canada is often explicitly compared to the United States where, it is almost always said, newcomers are expected to integrate and accommodate themselves to the dominant culture and language. Even when the comparison is not made explicitly, it is always implicit.

Canada's policy of official multiculturalism and the accompanying ethos of tolerance are taught to be morally superior to the putative American model. Again, even where this is not explicitly stated in a textbook or other curricular material, the message is clear and it is very likely to be expressed in unequivocal and even enthusiastic terms by elementary and high school teachers. Whether this message is correct is not the point. The fact that it relies in large part on a caricature of the United States that fails to see the ethnic diversity that exists in that country and the many ways in which this is recognized in public policy at all levels of government is important, but beside the point. The main point is that teaching about multiculturalism, and about Canadian values more generally, operates as a sort of soft, and sometimes not so soft, anti-Americanism. Canadian schoolchildren are taught what most will already have picked up at home and in the street, namely, that the United States is less tolerant and compassionate than Canada and therefore represents a morally and politically inferior model to its northern neighbor.

What is learned while young is reinforced in adulthood, particularly if one studies humanities or social sciences at a Canadian university. Several of the most influential contemporary interpreters of Canada construct a narrative of cultural differences that has embedded in it an argument for the superiority of Canadian values and institutions over those of the United States. In *Reflections of a Siamese Twin* (1998), John Ralston Saul offers a revisionist telling of Canadian history as a sort of deliberate and more or less successful attempt, going back to colonial times, to create a more collectivist, collaborative, group-based model of society, instead of the individualistic, assimilationist model to the south. Although Saul's book has been widely criticized by Canadian historians, its popularity does not depend on the historical veracity of the account Saul offers or on the credibility of the evidence that he adduces in support of this thesis. Saul tells a story that resonates with many Canadians, and especially with their opinion-leaders, because it makes them feel good – indeed rather superior – about themselves and their history.

Mark Kingwell's status as perhaps Canada's reigning pop philosopher rests in large measure on his ability to communicate a comforting image of Canadian moral superiority to the United States. "For generations," he says,

> we have been busy creating [in the shadow of the United States], a model of citizenship that is inclusive, diverse, open-ended and transnational. It is dedicated to far-reaching social justice and the rule of international law. . . . And we are successfully exporting it around the world.
>
> *(Kingwell 2003)*

It is not surprising that some of Canada's foremost philosophers, including Charles Taylor (1992), Will Kymlicka (2007), and James Tully (1995), are internationally known in large measure for their work on and advocacy of multiculturalism. Their respective writings on the Canadian experience with multiculturalism cannot be characterized as anti-American, in the way that George Grant's *Lament for a Nation* and *Technology and Empire* very clearly were. Grant's declaration that "[w]hen [Canadians] oblate themselves before 'the American way of life', they offer themselves on the altar of the reigning Western goddess" (Grant 1970, 54), is echoed in the early writings of Charles Taylor, written when he was a political activist in the 1960s (Taylor 1970). On the whole, however, and unlike the fulminations against American values, institutions and influence on Canada that was characteristic of the new Canadian nationalism that emerged in the 1960s and 1970s, Canada's philosophers of multiculturalism do not place reaction to "the reigning Western goddess" at the heart of their arguments for a Canadian identity and polity based on multiculturalism.

The image of Canada as culturally and morally superior to the United States is a staple of arts and humanities in Canadian universities. In 2016, the CBC interviewed students and professors on the campus of Toronto Metropolitan University, asking them what it meant to be Canadian and what they thought of the United States. "To be Canadian is to somehow live on a higher moral plane," was how the CBC journalist summarized their responses to the first question. In answer to the second question, students' responses included such descriptors as "ignorant," "discriminatory," "addicted to war," "pushy," "arrogant," "power-hungry," and "frenemies." Readers who wonder whether this might have been an unrepresentative group of young Canadians simply have not spent enough time on the country's university campuses (CBC News 2016).

Old Cultural Tropes Die Hard

American desires to annex Canada – real and imagined – have occupied an important place in the Canadian *imaginaire* since the 19th century. With the emergence of the new Canadian nationalism in the 1960s and 1970s, such beliefs experienced a resurgence not seen since the 1911 Canadian election and the dire predictions of annexation from the Conservative Party, Canadian manufacturing interests in Ontario and Quebec, and their allies in a cultural elite that was still very British in its leanings and therefore wary, to say the least, of anything that appeared to hold the promise of greater American influence in Canada and on Canadians.

These perceived dangers were reflected in a genre of Canadian fiction writing that arose at about the same time, a genre that might be described as *possession fantasies*. It may be seen in Margaret Atwood's early novel, *Surfacing* (1972), where the Americans in their powerboats tear apart the peace and harmony of Canadian nature. In *Surfacing*, it is money that enables Americans to possess, in a figurative way, their northern neighbor. But invasion and possession are more literal in a clutch of Canadian novels from the 1960s and 1970s that include Ray Smith's *Cape Breton is the Thought Control Center of Canada*, Ian Adam's *The Trudeau Papers*, and Richard Rohmer's bestselling books, *Annexation* and *Exoneration*. As the titles of Rohmer's books suggest, Canada is first taken over militarily by the United States, then manages a heroic liberation from the American invader. Valerie Broege's assessment of the possession fantasy embodied in Rohmer's books seems apt:

> [T]he popularity of Rohmer's [books] has much to do with tapping the resentment many Canadians feel in regard to America's greater power and aggressiveness. The novel[s] reflect the Canadian desire to see Uncle Sam get his comeuppance for going too far and assuming too much.
> *(Broege 1986, 34)*

What might be described as a soft version of the possession fantasy is found in the 1985 Canadian-made film, *My American Cousin* (Wilson 1985). Although only Canadians of a certain age and education are likely to have seen it – Canadian-made feature films seldom achieve wide commercial distribution – *My American Cousin* remains the classic Canadian film portrayal of America and of the relationship between these countries and their respective peoples.

The film is the story of Sandy, a young Canadian girl who longs for something different from the quiet, rather stifling routine of her life at "Paradise Ranch." The arrival of Butch, her American cousin, shatters this dull routine. His big red Cadillac, good looks, and disregard of the rules open a window onto a new world that seems to her far more exciting, sophisticated, and desirable than her own. In the end, however, Butch's parents arrive in their own oversized metal and chrome land yacht. His mother is irritated by what she sees as the backwoods tedium of the place and people to whom her wayward son fled, while Butch's father is impressed by the unrealized economic possibilities of the place. Butch returns home and Sandy is left with her quiet life and unsatisfied yearning.

My American Cousin captures beautifully the ambivalence that many Canadians have often felt toward the United States: a place where exciting things happen, where fortunes can be made, and whose culture and style are envied and avidly

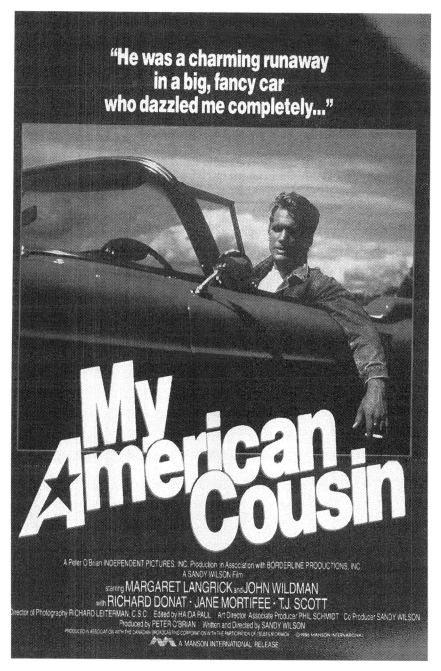

FIGURE 2.2   Sandra Wilson's 1985 film, "My American Cousin," captures the ambivalence that Canadians have long felt toward their rather overwhelming neighbor.
Courtesy of Okanagan Motion Picture Co.

consumed. But the rather overwhelming neighbor is also portrayed as shallowly materialistic, rapacious in its approach to nature, and morally inferior to Canada. Sandy admires her American cousin and thinks that she wants nothing more than to return with him to America. But she has doubts about his parents – "Those are your parents?" – doubts that even golden boy Butch – "Yeah, don't rub it in" – seems to share. Torn between desire for something that life in Canada seems unable to deliver and her inability to leave, it seems that Sandy may have to resign herself to the sensible if uneventful life of her mother.

The idea that America wishes to possess Canada, not through military means but through the fascination of their model and their apparent ability to buy all that they want, is expressed in a widely cited 1984 article by Margaret Atwood. So too is the conviction that there is virtue in resisting the seductions of the American suitor:

> [We share] the longest undefended backyard fence in the world. The Canadians are the folks in the neat little bungalow, with the tidy little garden and the duck pond. The Americans are the other folks, the ones in the sprawly mansion with the bad-taste statues on the lawn. There's a perpetual party; or something, going on there – loud music, raucous laughter, smoke billowing from the barbecue. Beer bottles and Coke cans land among the peonies.... Sometimes [Canadians] drop by next door, and find it exciting but scary. Sometimes the Americans drop by their house and find it clean. This worries the Canadians. They worry a lot. Maybe those Americans want to buy up their duck pond, with all the money they seem to have, and turn it into a cesspool or a water-skiing emporium.
>
> *(Atwood 1984)*

Over the next several years, Atwood would be one of the best-known voices in a phalanx of English-speaking Canada's foremost writers, artists, and broadcasters, opposing the free trade treaty signed in 1988 between Canada and the United States. Her opposition, and that of many other prominent figures in English Canada's cultural elite, was based principally on claims that Canadian values and culture would be threatened, and social programs undermined, by the proposed agreement. In more recent times, Atwood's book, *The Handmaid's Tale*, adapted for the screen by the streaming service Hulu in 2017, has reinforced her status as perhaps the foremost Canadian voice warning against what she has long seen as the dangerous tendencies in American culture. This dystopian story portrays Canada as a place of refuge for those fleeing exploitation, thus evoking images of the Underground Railway during the era of slavery, but also suggesting that Canada, unlike the United States, is a place of freedom and safety where the exploited can rebuild their lives.

Along with Maude Barlow, Mel Hurtig, David Suzuki, Farley Mowat, Pierre Berton, Margaret Laurence, and other prominent members of the Canadian cultural and media elites, Atwood was a founding member of The Council of Canadians. Created in 1985, the Council spearheaded opposition to the proposal of free trade with the United States. In addition to their dire predictions that free trade would accelerate the economic takeover of Canada by American capital, undermine political sovereignty, and lead inevitably to the emaciation of Canadian more generous social programs, the Council's spokespersons predicted that Canada's cultural autonomy and distinctiveness would be jeopardized. The country's 1988 federal election was fought mainly on the issue of free trade with the United States.

It is not necessary to try to judge whether the claims made in opposition to or in support of free trade were more plausible at that time, let alone whether history has vindicated one side or the other. What is relevant to the current analysis is that the anti-free trade arguments drew heavily on a deep well of Canadian nationalist fears of American annexation. Prominent Canadians and organizations that supported free trade, from Conservative Prime Minister Brian Mulroney on down, were portrayed as willingly and even enthusiastically complicit in the final step in the process that George Grant had lamented two decades earlier. Given that among the three national parties that polled any significant number of votes in the 1988 election, the two anti-free trade parties – the Liberal Party and the New Democratic Party – outpolled the victorious pro-free trade Conservative Party by a margin of 52 to 43 percent, one might be inclined to conclude that the Canadian electorate agreed. But as prominent as the free trade issue was in this election, as it was back in 1911, it was not a referendum. It would, therefore, be baseless to conclude that all voters cast their ballots according to their views on this issue.

What is clear is that the Canadian electorate was divided on this issue. A significant share of the public, even if they did not accept the annexation narrative that was heard so often leading up to and during the 1988 election campaign, did not support greater integration between Canada and the United States. But a significant share did (Janigan 1988). Canadian ambivalence toward their country's relationship to the United States was once again on full display.

No discussion of how Canadians have viewed their southern neighbor is complete without mention of the very popular CBC current affairs comedy program, *The Mercer Report* (2004–18). It featured a segment called "Talking to Americans." The premise was simple: comedian Rick Mercer represented himself as a Canadian journalist and presented unsuspecting Americans with preposterous claims about Canada. The popularity of "Talking to Americans" across generations of viewers rested on Canadians' well-founded belief that most Americans are woefully ignorant of Canada and on the sense of resentment that this has always inspired. Mercer transformed this resentment into humor; humor that enabled Canadians to feel superior to the gullible, rather stupid-seeming Americans who appeared to believe in the plausibility of such false claims as Canada's national legislature being an igloo – the Canada National Igloo – that Tim Horton (the name of the country's most popular donut chain) was the name of the prime minister, and that many Canadians finally wanted to abolish their country's tradition of placing seniors on ice flows and leaving them to perish.

At the same time, however, and consistent with the ambivalence that has long characterized the Canadian image of America, Canadians who express a smug and confident disdain for American values and institutions are often the first in line to take advantage of career opportunities in the United States. Based on the hundreds of interviews that Jeffrey Simpson did for his book *Star-Spangled Canadians* (Simpson 2000), it seems that many Canadians who have left for jobs and economic opportunities – while usually lamenting the fact that they could not find the same opportunities at home and continuing to feel warmly toward Canada – also prefer aspects of the American culture and lifestyle. A former editor for a Canadian literary magazine, Tajja Issen, writes about what she characterizes as the ceiling on creative opportunities in Canada that ensures that making it in the United States is still, as it has long been, the litmus test that one is truly good in his or her line of work. Comparing the life of a creative professional in Toronto to New York, she writes,

> Toronto's energy flows endlessly toward the impulse to win, to never stop working until you hit your head on the visible ceiling. Then you work some more. New York has that vibe too, maybe even more so, but I feel like everyone's more self-aware about it. And, more importantly, there's no ceiling. You can try to dominate the world and touch the clouds, but the world is so vast it would obviously be foolish to try.
>
> *(Isen 2022)*

This is very much the same mixture of admiration and envy that Nova Scotia politician Joseph Howe expressed in 1854 after dining with John Quincy Adams and other members of the American elite. It was and still is a sense that horizons are vaster and opportunities greater in the United States.

American Decline, the Rise of Trumpism, and Canadians' Image of America

The last decade, and particularly the years since the 2016 election of Donald Trump as president of the United States, have seen a proliferation of articles in Canada with such titles as "Searching for the American Dream? Go to Canada" (Khanna 2021), "The American Dream Has Moved to Canada" (Gilmore 2017), "The 'Canadian Dream': Has It Overtaken the American Dream?" and "It's Official, Canadians Now Make More Money than Americans" (Howse 2019). As we will see in the next chapter, very similar analyses also have proliferated in the United States. But American contributions to this story of role reversal take the form of laments of what has been lost and how to recover the promise of the American Dream for Americans, whereas those from Canada tend to celebrate Canada's achievements and what is seen as proof that the Canadian model is superior to that of the United States. By the end of the Trump presidency, the self-congratulatory mood of many Canadians when they looked south was joined by something rather new: pity. They were not alone in experiencing this unfamiliar sentiment (Earle 2020; McTague 2020).

To be clear, the belief among many Canadians and their opinion-leaders that America is in decline and that Canada offers the world a better path toward the ideals that were once associated most closely with the United States is not something that began with the election of Donald Trump. A 1986 editorial in the Toronto *Globe & Mail* expressed what was already a fairly widespread sentiment:

> We do not turn to the United States as a model of social justice or even intelligent self-interest when it comes to domestic policy. Far from it . . . . America is not the ideal . . . in many of the civilized aspects of life, though the dynamism of the U.S. economy is impressive and attractive. America pays too little attention to the community.
>
> *(Globe and Mail 1986)*

Always avid consumers of news from the United States, Canadians' views about what many of them have long seen as the multiple crises of American society – including racial conflict, a gun-related homicide rate without equal among democracies, growing economic inequality, and political polarization – have been reinforced by events over the past couple of decades. Many if not most Canadians also believe, as is true of the populations of most western democracies including that of the United States, that America's global influence is in decline and that this is not likely to be reversed, regardless of which party controls the White House.[10]

There is no "Canadian view" on whether and how declining American influence abroad and increasing trouble at home matter for Canada. While polls have shown for many years, predating the Trump presidency, that a preponderance of Canadians subscribe to the notion of American declinism, a significant minority does not. Moreover, according to surveys taken during and after the Trump presidency, about one in five Canadians believe that Canada is better off with Trump in the White House (Angus Reid 2022, 7).

Nevertheless, there is not much doubt that among both Canadian opinion-leaders and the general public, anxiety in recent years about the consequences of American domestic politics for Canada has been widespread. That anxiety was on full display during the Trump presidency, reaching higher levels after the Capitol Hill riots of January 6, 2021, in which Trump was complicit. It did not abate once it became apparent that the reelection of Donald Trump in 2024 was by no means out of the question. Media stories with such titles as "Canada should be preparing for the end of American democracy" (Danisch 2022), "The American polity is cracked and might collapse" (Homer-Dixon 2022), "Is the U.S. heading towards civil war?" (Paikin 2022), and "Angst of the Americas: Four-in-five Canadians worry about the domestic impacts of continued U.S. political turmoil" (Angus Reid 2022) were not uncommon after Trump's reluctant departure from the White House.

In an op-ed published two weeks before the assault on Capitol Hill in Canada's most influential newspaper, the *Globe and Mail*, Canadian political scientist Thomas Homer-Dixon wrote, "By 2025, American democracy could collapse,

FIGURE 2.3   The image of the United States as a "mobocracy" already existed in Canada in the late 19th century. It resurfaced toward the end of the Trump presidency when what many Canadians perceived to be their neighbor's unruly response to the COVID-19 pandemic and the political divisions that led to the January 6, 2021, assault on Capitol Hill seemed to confirm this image.

Courtesy of Patrick Corrigan.

causing extreme domestic political instability, including widespread civil violence. . . . By 2030, if not sooner the country could be governed by a right-wing dictatorship" (Homer-Dixon 2022). David Frum, a prominent Canadian writer and political commentator who is best known as an analyst of the American political scene and a former speechwriter for President George W. Bush, had already made similarly dire predictions in his 2018 book, *Trumpocracy: The Corruption of the American Republic*.

Canadians and their opinion-leaders have not been alone in expressing such fears about the consequences of growing polarization in American society, going back to before the election of Donald Trump. But the issue resonates in particular ways in Canada because of the scale and intimacy of the country's ties to the

United States. This was seen in the winter of 2022, when a self-described "Freedom Convoy" of Canadian truck drivers and their supporters staged protests in a number of Canadian cities, most notably in Ottawa. The protesters were expressing their opposition to the Canadian government's requirement that truckers entering Canada from the United States – and about 30,000 of them do so on an average day – be fully vaccinated against the coronavirus. As their signs, banners and the words of their spokespersons made clear, their opposition extended more generally to mandatory vaccinations, lockdowns, and the other regulations imposed in response to the COVID-19 pandemic.

The protesters' narrative of civil disobedience against COVID-19 restrictions that had gone too far and for too long was immediately countered by another that was offered by the Canadian government and many opinion-leaders. It alleged that the money in support of the protesters, and some of the leadership and organization of the protests, originated in the United States, concerns that the Canadian Prime Minister expressed directly to Joe Biden in a telephone conversation during the protesters' three-week blockade of the Parliament Hill area of Ottawa. In short, the protests – the scale and duration of which were quite unusual for Canada – represented the importation of American right-wing extremism (Ling 2022).

The trope of American interference in Canadian politics has roots that go back at least to the 1963 federal election. Claims were made (with some foundation) that the Kennedy administration aided in engineering the defeat of the Conservative government of John Diefenbaker (Bourque and Martin 2013; Canadian Press 2015). In 1995, when the province of Quebec held a referendum on whether it should separate from Canada, the administration of Bill Clinton approached the Canadian government to ask whether the president's public intervention in support of Canadian unity would be welcome.[11] More recently, an Elections Canada report on the 2015 Canadian election acknowledged that money from American anti-oil organizations was channeled to Canadian groups that opposed the reelection of the Conservative government and its candidates (Postmedia News 2017). Moreover, American-based environmental groups have been active for many years in supporting the anti-pipeline movement in Canada (Hunt 2019). In short, the narrative of an invisible American hand in the protests that brought Canada's capital to a halt for three weeks in the winter of 2022 was made against a backdrop of past claims of American interference in Canadian politics. Such claims seem entirely plausible to many Canadians, predisposed as they are toward the idea that the United States is, or at least has the capacity to act as a sort of *éminence grise* in their country's politics and that American domestic politics may provide the motivation to do so.

The Trump presidency amplified concerns that many Canadians and some of their leaders have long expressed about American decline on the global stage. Their reasoning has gone roughly like this: if American influence in the world, particularly economic but also political influence, is declining, while that of other countries and regions, including China, the Asia-Pacific region more generally, India, and the EU (this thesis has also included the BRICS group of countries at various points over the past couple of decades), then Canada should reduce its dependence on the United States and develop more robust ties to these newer centers of world power. A "smaller America" on which Canada's prosperity at home and influence abroad depends is not in the interests of Canadians. Writing in 2016, as he was assuming his new role as a foreign policy advisor to Prime Minister Justin Trudeau, Roland Paris wrote, "No longer can the United States be relied upon either to drive Canadian economic growth or to single-handedly underwrite the global trading system and international security" (Paris 2016, 1).

It is important to recognize that this view has had significant traction in Canada, particularly on the center-left of the political spectrum, even before the election of Donald Trump. The recalibration of American engagement abroad that took place under President Obama, partly in reaction to the interventionist policies of the previous Bush administration, had already signaled a shift toward a more restrained view of American power. This coincided with a steady stream of media commentary, in Canada as elsewhere, on the rise of China as the world's foremost economic power.

At the same time, and consistent with the ambivalence that has always characterized Canadians' perceptions of their southern neighbor, any evidence that Canada appeared to be losing influence with the American government and that the "special relationship" that many Canadians and their opinion-leaders had come to think was a given of the Canada–US bilateral relationship was greeted with dismay. This dismay reached depths not seen since the famously strained relationship between President Kennedy and Prime Minister Diefenbaker in the early 1960s, when it became clear that Canada would not receive an exemption from the protectionist policies that were a pillar of Trump's "Make America Great Again" agenda. It is fair to say that most Canadians, including those who were never convinced that the closeness implicit in the idea of the special relationship was in Canada's interests, were shocked at the disdain that the Trump administration frequently showed toward their country. They were in for another surprise when, after the election of Joe Biden in 2020 and the Democratic Party's control of Congress, the protectionism did not abate. The insults were gone, but there were few tangible signs that Canada was seen by Washington decision-makers as a partner deserving of special treatment.

Conclusion

Canadians have long been aware of the truth of Pierre Trudeau's often-cited remark that living next to the United States is like sharing a bed with an elephant, "No matter how friendly and even-tempered is the beast, if I can call it that, one is affected by every twitch and grunt" (Trudeau 1969). This awareness is an important part of their image of America and of the very asymmetrical relationship that exists between Canada and the United States. It is also part of the ambivalence that Canadians and their leaders feel toward the United States, some of them believing that the solution is to get out of the bed or at least to create more distance from the elephant. Others believe that geography and history are destiny and that Canada has no option but to make the best of the country's extensive economic, security, and cultural ties to the

United States. As we will see in Chapter 4, the tension between these very different perspectives has had major impacts on Canadian government policies.

Notes

1. Canadian history has been interpreted quite differently by the country's French- and English-speaking historians. See Marcel Trudel and Geneviève Laloux-Jain, *Canadian History Textbooks: A Comparative Study*. Study for the Royal Commission on Bilingualism and Biculturalism (Ottawa: Government of Canada, 1970).
2. Chapter XI of *Roughing It in the Bush* provides a good distillation of Susanna Moodie's thoughts on this subject. Her observations and conclusions are quite similar to those arrived at by Frances Trollope in her *Domestic Manners of the Americans*, published in 1832.
3. In his meticulously documented history of Upper Canada (Ontario) during the first half of the 19th century, Fred Landon shows that the War of 1812 was a watershed after which a sort of official anti-Americanism was promoted by colonial authorities that were mistrustful of the loyalties of a population in which a majority had been born in the United States. Their solution was to actively encourage greater immigration from the British Isles and, indeed, Britain became the major source of immigration to Upper Canada by the 1820s. But this anti-Americanism did not emerge organically from the population of British North America. Rather it was part of a deliberate policy pursued by the colonial elites in order to reduce the influence of Americans and American values, particularly in Upper Canada.
4. British historian Ged Martin points out, "In each of the first four decades after Confederation, the *increase* in the population of the United States alone was twice the number of Canadians." In the face of such numbers, and the much greater attractiveness of the United States than Canada during this era, Martin suggests that it is little wonder that the image that Canadians and their leaders had of their neighbor was fueled by insecurity. At the same time, he argues that the survival and development of a distinct Canadian identity ought to be seen as evidence of strength, rather than weakness, in the face of rather formidable odds. See Martin (2004, 204).
5. When the Treaty was abrogated in 1866, it was not because of British or colonial dissatisfaction. It was due mainly to political rather than economic reasons on the American side of the border, where there was great resentment in the North toward Britain's unofficial, but clear support for the South during the Civil War. See Laughlin and Willis, *Reciprocity*, pp. 58–59.
6. Canada would acquire the constitutional authority to sign international treaties in its own right in an evolutionary manner, beginning with the 1919 Treaty of Versailles and the 1923 Halibut Treaty with the United States, not achieving unlimited sovereignty in such matters in 1947.
7. D.H. Lawrence expressed these misgivings more succinctly than any of his contemporaries in his short poem, "The Evening Land," published in November 1922.
8. The Canadian Radio Broadcasting Commission was created in 1932 with the support of both the Conservative government and the Liberal opposition. It was transformed into a crown corporation called the CBC in 1936. The NFB was created in 1939.
9. I am grateful for Jan Raska's research (Raska 2020), on which this paragraph depends.
10. In 2008, 35 percent of Canadians named the United States as the world's leading economic power, compared to 37 percent who said it was China. By 2020, 36 percent said the United States and 47 percent named China. Pew, Global Attitudes Project. An Angus Reid poll carried out just over a year after Joe Biden's 2021 inauguration found that six of ten Canadians believed that his reelection in 2024 would make the United States worse off [28%] or no better [33%].
11. The answer was yes, and the support was duly given. This story is confirmed by then US ambassador to Canada, James Blanchard in his book, *Behind the Embassy Door*.

3
CANADA

From Existential Threat to the Unknown Country

Introduction

Canadians' obsession with America is long-standing and understandable. Their image of America always has been crucial to their own sense of national identity. Comparison between their country and the United States comes to them quite readily, indeed, often inevitably. On such subjects as health care, policing, race relations, access to post-secondary education, economic inequality, immigration, and the proper balance between soft and hard power in world affairs, Canadians will usually have an opinion – informed or otherwise – on what distinguishes them from their southern neighbors.

None of this is true when it comes to the American image of Canada. Most Americans, most of the time, devote little thought to Canada and its people. Their sense of national identity, more buffeted and contested in recent decades than during much of the 20th century, rarely includes Canada as a point of reference. Comparison between their society and the United Kingdom, Germany France, or certain other countries seems to come more easily than to the place immediately next door. At the same time, it is clear that many Americans have not been in the habit of comparing their country, its institutions, and its policies to other countries: period (Zakaria 2011).

This enormous difference in the intensity and frequency – a stare versus an occasional glance – of the Canadian gaze toward the other is an important aspect of the asymmetry that characterizes their relationship. No American has ever thought of writing a book with the title, "The Unknown Country" (Hutchison 1942), in which he attempts to describe and explain his country to Canadians. That was, however, the title of the Canadian journalist Bruce Hutchison's 1942 book, the intended market for which was an American readership. As it turned out, sales in

DOI: 10.4324/9781032675220-3

the United States were unimpressive, but the book did very well in the Canadian market. Forty years later, the Canadian writer Pierre Berton took on the same challenge with his book, *Why We Act Like Canadians*, written as a series of letters to an American friend named Sam. The fate of Berton's 1982 book was the same as Hutchison's. It proved to be quite popular in Canada, but outside of a rather small circle of professional Canadianists (mainly professors of Canadian studies at American universities), it went unnoticed in the country to which the explanations of Canada were ostensibly addressed.

Americans, it seems, do not know very much about Canada and are not motivated to learn about their neighbor. This is, however, an overly simplistic and rather misleading assessment of the American image of Canada and Canadians. It requires four important qualifications. First, the American view of Canada has mattered, even quite a lot, at certain moments in the shared history of these countries. Second, it has always been the case that some Americans have paid keen attention to Canada and that their informed views, notwithstanding being held by a small fraction of the population, have occasionally had a disproportionate impact on US–Canada relations. Third, even though the American public has seldom paid much attention or had much knowledge of Canada, their interests and sentiments, as these relate to Canada and as they have been perceived by American policy-makers, have sometimes played a role in bilateral relations between these countries. Fourth, the image or competing images of Canada held by American opinion-leaders, particularly in recent decades, have sometimes become part of the domestic political conversation in the United States, refracted through ideological divisions in that society.

All of this adds up to an image of the other that has been, as we will see in Chapter 4, less consequential for American politics and policy than the image of America has been in Canada. And yet, at least in the early history of the American republic, the image of Canada was a significant driver of politics. Indeed, Canada was seen by many as an existential threat to the United States.

The Threat from the North

It is easy to forget that there were 20 North American colonies at the time of the Declaration of Independence. Thirteen rejected British rule, but seven did not. The combined population of the Thirteen Colonies was vastly greater than that of those that remained loyal to Britain (roughly 2.5 million to approximately 100,000 during the 1770s) (Statistics Canada n.d.; United States Census Bureau 2022). Nevertheless, British troops remained in these colonies and, despite their defeat of the British in the Revolutionary War, it would be quite some time before Americans and their leaders would be confident that British influence operating through Canada did not represent a threat to their sovereign territory and to their country's expansion.

It is important to keep in mind that what Americans referred to as Canada in the 18th and 19th centuries was thought of as an outpost of British policies and interests in North America. This perception was accurate and did not change very much even after the colonies of the United Canadas (Ontario and Quebec), Nova Scotia, and New Brunswick formed the semi-sovereign Dominion of Canada in 1867.[1] The new state thus created was viewed, and with good reason, as part of the British Empire. As such, and at that moment in time, it did not have its own voice in international affairs. The shadow cast by British control over Canada until the adoption in 1848 of self-government for domestic affairs in the colonies, and continuing British influence over foreign affairs until the early 20th century, meant that what historian Gordon Stewart calls the "American response to Canada" (Stewart 1992), was largely a response to Britain. It had relatively little to do with the Canadian people and how they were perceived from the southern side of the border.

Consequently, when Stewart writes, "The United States and Canada began as bad neighbors," and that, "for the first seventy or so years after independence, the American response to Canada was characterized by suspicion and hostility" (Stewart 1992, 23), this needs to be understood in the context of what was an era of British control over Canada. The image of Canada, certainly among American politicians and opinion-leaders, had roots that were both ideological and geo-strategic.

Ideologically, Canada represented the social order and system of government that American colonists had rejected. The reasons they gave for this rejection are set forth in the second paragraph of the Declaration of Independence and in the list of 27 "abuses and usurpations" of which the British authorities are accused in that document. Inspired by the natural rights philosophy of John Locke,[2] the principles invoked to justify revolution, and on which the US Constitution drafted in 1787 would rest, included consent of the people as the sole legitimate basis for government (a corollary of which was the idea that the elected legislature was the first branch of government, as Madison would put it in Federalist 51); limits on the powers of government, particularly in regard to individual rights and freedoms; and the equal right of citizens to life, liberty, and the pursuit of happiness. The role of government – again, pure Locke – was to protect individuals in the enjoyment of these rights, including their right to property. Egregious failure to do so might warrant revolution. Finally, although not specifically mentioned in the Declaration of Independence or in the Constitution ratified in 1789, protection for religious freedom and the separation of church and state (understood at the time as an end to state religions, such as the Church of England in the some of the southern states and the Congregational Church in most of the northern ones) was a contested, but ultimately accepted principle of the American model, enshrined in the First Amendment.

On every one of these counts, the American model was antithetical to the ideas and practices of the British colonial authorities. In the decades following the War of Independence, American political leaders were keenly aware that those who governed the Canadian colonies were determined to maintain the authority of the crown, embodied in the person of the British-appointed governor-general of each colony, limit the powers of the elected colonial assemblies, continue the privileged status of the Church of England (and that of the Catholic Church in Quebec under the Quebec Act 1774), and place severe restrictions on the press. The British colonial authorities in Canada also regulated the expansion of settlement through their control over the system for the sale of crown land. Indeed, the British model of territorial expansion was premised on the orderly and controlled settlement of the colonial territories to which Britain laid claim. To permit otherwise would be to risk the authorities' ability to govern territories in which settlement ran ahead of such outposts of state authority as forts and public officials. This ran counter to the American practice, which preceded independence, of largely unregulated westward movement of persons.

Defeating Britain in the War of Independence did not put an end to the ideological system that the American colonists had rejected. It simply moved it to the borders of the United States. American mistrust of British actions and intentions on the North American continent continued after the signing in 1783 of the Treaty of Paris. It was natural enough that these sentiments should be projected onto Canada, with which the new republic shared roughly four thousand miles of border – much of it disputed – to the north and to the west. In the words of Robert Livingston, a delegate to the Continental Congress and the US Minister to France between 1801 and 1804[3] "[Canada is] a martial Colony containing every means of attack" (quoted in Stewart 1992, 27). Livingston's assessment of the Canadian geo-strategic menace, communicated to the French foreign minister in 1803, was widely shared among his contemporaries. While limited to a mistrust of the mother country held by most Americans, in some cases, it assumed a more extreme form that involved what historian Lawrence Peskin refers to as conspiratorial anglophobia. "[C]onspiratorial anglophobes," he writes, "believed, or purported to believe, that behind Britain's disparate anti-American actions and policies . . . loomed a larger, well-orchestrated plot to recolonize the United States" (Peskin 2011, 647). This belief was, Peskin argues, a key unifying element for the Democratic-Republican Party of Thomas Jefferson during the first couple of decades of the 19th century.

Although the attribution of a grand design on the part of Britain for the retaking of all or parts of the United States, using Canada as a staging ground, was perhaps unfounded, there certainly was no shortage of British actions to fuel Americans' mistrust. Among them were the British failure to abandon forts that, under the terms of the Treaty of Paris, were located on land that was American territory, abundant evidence of the British colonial authorities encouraging and supporting Indian attacks on American settlements and forts, and some evidence of espionage that was orchestrated from Canada. Whether this amounted to a grand design is moot, but there is no doubt that it represented a policy that went back to the pre-revolutionary era and that was one of the key drivers of revolt against British rule, namely the aim of limiting the territory of the United States.

After its defeat by the Continental Army (with, it must be acknowledged, the significant and perhaps even decisive military support of French troops and naval vessels), Britain maintained thousands of troops in the British North American colonies. At the outbreak of the War of 1812, it had about 10,000 military regulars in the Canadian colonies, a number that rose quickly during that war. This may appear to be a rather small number, particularly when one considers that the population of the United States in 1812 had reached roughly 7.7 million, compared to about half a million persons in the British North American colonies. But because of lingering mistrust of a standing army in preference for state militias that were typically poorly trained and under-armed, there were only about 5,000–6,000 American professional soldiers at the outbreak of the War of 1812. This number would increase to about 38,000 later in the conflict (Skelton 1994, 3), compared to about 58,000 British regulars by the end of the war.

The view of Canada as a persistent and serious geo-strategic threat was an important part of the backdrop to the War of 1812, at the time referred to by some as America's second war of independence and by historian Alan Taylor as "the final act of the American Revolution" (Taylor n.d.). As Reginald Horsman writes,

> To understand the causes of the War of 1812 it is necessary to focus in detail on the events from 1803 to 1812; but, to understand American attitudes toward Canada in that war it is necessary to understand American fears about the British in Canada that had existed since the Revolution, American dreams of a continent free of British influence and dominated by the United States, and the course of American arguments regarding Canada during the War of 1812.
>
> *(Horsman 1987, 2)*

Thomas Jefferson's famously inaccurate prediction that the conquest of Canada "will be a mere matter of marching," reflected the view that the war would be the occasion for the end of this long-standing menace to the security of the United States. This view was shared by many of Jefferson's compatriots.

But only part of the prediction proved to be true. Canada was not annexed. Nevertheless, the end of the War of 1812, which was a sort of military stalemate, marked the beginning of the end of the American image of Canada as a threat to American territory and as a staging ground for the reintroduction in the United States or across the western territories of North America of the British model of governance and society. The war's outcome, writes Stewart, "gave birth to a new sense of confidence that the young, decentralized republic – with no permanent military establishment on the scale of the European powers – could organize effectively to protect their rights and their territory" (Stewart 1992, 30).

A direct consequence of this new sense of confidence was a decline in the importance that Canada occupied in the minds of Americans and their leaders. The Royal Proclamation of 1763 had prohibited population expansion west of the Appalachian Mountains. By 1840 about seven million persons, representing about 40 percent of the total American population, lived west of Appalachia. The old fear that Britain, operating through Canada and its alliances with Native Americans, would block the westward expansion of the United States evaporated following the War of 1812.

FIGURE 3.1 British troops burned down the White House, the Capitol Building, and other government buildings when they captured Washington in 1814. The end of the War of 1812 would also mark the end of American fears of Canada as a staging ground for the perceived threat from Great Britain.

Image from Benson John Lossing, ed. *Harper's Encyclopedia of United States History*. Vol. 10, New York, NY: Harper and Brothers 1912.

The Early American Image of Les Canadiens and the Canadian People

While security concerns loomed large in shaping the American image of Canada from the Revolution until the early 19th century, there also emerged during this period various ideas about the people of Canada. Less precise and less consequential than the image of Canada as a security threat, some of these early ideas about Canadians would persist for quite some time. Indeed, certain among them continue to exist.

One of the first of these involved *les canadiens*, the French-speaking Catholic population of New France, which fell under British control in 1759 and was formally ceded to Britain in 1763 under the Treaty of Paris. Catholicism was quite rare in the Thirteen Colonies.[4] More significantly, it would be looked upon with suspicion as an anti-democratic and fundamentally un-American faith well after millions of Catholics immigrated to the United States in the mid- and late-19th centuries. The fact that *les canadiens* spoke French and lived under a social system – the seigneurial system of land ownership that created a hierarchy of rights and obligations between the seigneurs and the tenants who worked their land – that was feudal and fundamentally undemocratic, was almost certainly less important in the eyes of early Americans than their Catholicism. It was assumed that they would be happy to be rid of feudalism and that their language would soon be discarded like an old suit of clothes. Religion was another matter.

Nonetheless, the *canadiens*' status as a conquered people under the rule of English-speaking protestants who pledged loyalty to the British crown led Washington, Franklin, and other leading figures of the revolutionary era to believe that the French-speaking, Catholic people of Quebec might prefer to join in revolt against British rule. In his Address to the Inhabitants of Canada, dated September 14, 1775, George Washington writes:

> [The British] have persuaded themselves, they have even dared to say, that the Canadians were not capable of distinguishing between the Blessings of Liberty, and the Wretchedness of Slavery; that gratifying the Vanity of a little Circle of Nobility – would blind the Eyes of the People of Canada . . . .
>
> Come then, my Brethren, unite with us in an indissoluble Union, let us run together to the same Goal. – We have taken up Arms in Defence of our Liberty, our Property, our Wives, and our Children, we are determined to preserve them, or die. We look forward with Pleasure to that Day not far remote (we hope) when the Inhabitants of America shall have one Sentiment, and the full Enjoyment of the Blessings of a free Government. . . .
>
> The Grand American Congress have sent an Army into your Province, under the Command of General Schuyler; not to plunder, but to protect you; to animate, and bring forth into Action those Sentiments of Freedom you have disclosed, and which the Tools of Despotism would extinguish through the whole Creation.
>
> *(Washington 1775)*

A delegation that included Benjamin Franklin was commissioned by the Continental Congress in 1776 to visit Canada in the hope of winning support for revolt against British rule. As William Riddell writes, "[T]he Clergy . . . remained firm in their allegiance to the British Crown. Nothing but very strong reasons could induce the Laity to decline to follow their Clergy: and no such reason ever appeared" (Riddel 1924, 142). *Les canadiens* had no particular affection for their British rulers, as demonstrated by their unwillingness to fight with the British when American forces invaded Canada. But the republican arguments of Washington, Franklin, and others, added to their awareness of the deep prejudice against Roman Catholicism in the Thirteen Colonies, inclined them to remain on the sidelines.

This was not surprising. The Continental Congress had referred to the protection for the Catholic religion in the Quebec Act, 1774 as "subversive of American rights" and condemned the Act for "establishing the Roman Catholic religion in the Province of Quebec" (cited in Riddell 1924, 118). The extent of the American colonists' mistrust and even hatred of the Catholic religion was on full display a month later when, on October 21, 1774, the Continental Congress adopted an Address to the People of Great Britain that included this attack on the Quebec Act:

> Canada is to be so extended, modelled and governed as that by being disunited from us, detached from our interests by civil and religious prejudices, that by their numbers daily swelling with Catholic Emigrants from Europe . . . they may become formidable to us and on occasion be fit instruments in the hands of power to reduce the ancient free Protestant Colonies to the same state of slavery with themselves.
>
> *(cited in Riddell 1924, 19)*

Indeed, the Quebec Act is included along with the four "Intolerable Acts" passed by the British Parliament in 1774, as having collectively triggered the American Revolution. The particularly offensive provision of the Quebec Act was that which increased enormously the territory of the colony of Quebec, extending it to include the lands on the western frontier of the Thirteen Colonies. Many colonists feared that this vast territory, in which the status of the Roman Catholic faith was recognized and protected, might be dominated by people whose religious beliefs were seen as antithetical to freedom and Protestantism. This was clearly and even virulently expressed by the Continental Congress's characterization of Catholicism as a religion that had "dispersed impiety, bigotry, persecution, murder and rebellion through every part of the world" (Continental Congress 1774).

A rather more intellectual portrayal of the *canadiens* was provided by the great American historian Francis Parkman in his enormously influential *France and England in North America* (Parkman 1892). More than any other historian, Parkman's writings on the pre-Conquest era in New France would be accepted as authoritative throughout the English-speaking world until well into the 20th century. The notion of the Canadian society as priest-ridden and thoroughgoingly illiberal finds ample support in his work. "The Canadian priests held the manners of the colony under a rule as rigid as that of the Puritan churches of New England," he writes (Chapter XIX). Parkman acknowledges that the population was often restive under such social control, but he argues that the illiberal character of the Canadian people, its unfittedness for democratic governance, was not due only to the influence of the church and the French colonial authorities. Their history and culture did not prepare them for the age of freedom, announced by the American and French revolutions. This was reinforced, Parkman says, after the British conquest of New France. With their state and civil elites deposed by the British, there was left only the French-speaking clerical elite. It became, he says, "the guardians of order throughout Canada" (Chapter XXI). Parkman agrees with his American compatriots that this was not a salutary development. In perhaps, the most famous words from "The Old Regime in Canada," Parkman writes, "England imposed on Canada the boon of rational and ordered liberty. . . . A happier calamity never befell a people than the conquest of Canada by the British arms" (Chapter XXI).

Parkman's assessment was echoed by Henry David Thoreau and by most other American travelers who wrote about their travels to Canada. Indeed, the prevailing image of Canada was that of a rather quaint, somewhat backward and Old World place, lacking the vitality and individualism of America. Sometimes this comparison was clearly unfavorable. "In Canada," wrote Henry David Thoreau after a visit to Quebec City, "you are reminded of the government every day. It parades itself before you. It is not content to be the servant, but will be the master" (Thoreau 1866, 77–78). Thoreau's image of Canada, as Patrick Lacroix argues, was very much rooted in what by then were well-established tropes about French-speaking Canada. Slavish in their orientation toward the authority of both the state and the Catholic church, the *canadiens* were seen as a people unfit for and even hostile toward democracy (Lacroix 2017).

This view gained strength toward the end of the 19th century as a result of the migration to the New England states, particularly Maine and Massachusetts, of hundreds of thousands of French-speaking Quebecers who sought work in the mill towns of this region. They were inclined to be seen and feared as a culturally foreign element. By the 1880s, writes David Vermette, "elite American newspapers, including the *New York Times*, saw a sinister plot afoot. The Catholic Church, they said, had dispatched French Canadian workers southward in a bid to seize control of New England" (Vermette 2019). An 1881 article in the *New York Times* warned that these immigrants were, "ignorant and unenterprising, subservient to the most bigoted class of Catholic priests in the world. . . . They care nothing for our free institutions, have no desire for civil or religious liberty or the benefits of education" (quoted in Vermette 2019). Long-standing and widely share tropes about popery, that alleged "a priestly scheme now fervently fostered in Canada for the purpose of bringing New-England under the control of the Roman Catholic faith" (ibid.), were common (Chamberlain 1884).

This very negative, indeed, paranoid view of French Canadians' Catholic influence and purpose in the United States was pushed aside for a brief time in the late 1830s to the early 1840s after an unsuccessful rebellion in Quebec, at the time named Lower Canada. George Bancroft, perhaps the preeminent American historian of the 19th century, interpreted the rebellion of the *patriotes* against the British authorities in Lower Canada as having been driven by an outmoded "colonial & mercantile system . . . near its change" (quoted in Marshall 1990, 306), and that parallels between the American Revolution and the dissent and resistance that occurred in Lower Canada were facile. Many American politicians and opinion-leaders saw the matter differently, however, and were inclined to see in Louis-Joseph Papineau, a self-proclaimed republican, the spirit and aims of their own revolutionary leaders.[5] The accounts that appeared in the American press at the time were filtered through the lens of America's own experience with undemocratic governance. "Everything was read through the spectrum of American experience" (Stewart 1992, 43), writes Gordon Stewart. He attributes this to what he characterizes as "widespread American ignorance of conditions in Canada" (Stewart 1992, 47).

FIGURE 3.2   The Old South Church in Bath, Maine, was set afire by Americans. They viewed the French Canadian Catholics who worshipped there as a popish influence whose intent was to subvert American values and institutions.

John Hilling, "Burning of Old South Church, Bath, Maine, c.1854," Courtesy National Gallery of Art, Washington.

Even when the perception of French-speaking and Catholic Canada was not negative, there was a tendency to romanticize and certainly to interpret matters through an American lens. Articles in the popular monthly publications of the 19th century, including *Harper's*, *Scribner's*, and *The Atlantic Monthly*, occasionally included what might be described as traveler's accounts or even tourist guide pieces that tended to characterize as Quebec as picaresque, quaint, and foreign in a non-threatening way, and to portray its people as friendly but rather simple and even backward in their ways. This description of the Canadian habitant, published in *Harper's* in 1883, is not untypical of the genre:

The [habitant's] character is in harmony with his external existence – simple-minded, ignorant, virtuous, austere, and courteous. Canada is our twin brother in chronology and geography; and yet no other contiguous lands differ more widely. You can scarcely believe yourself in this age when you pass from our luxurious, elaborate, and practical existence to the poor, primitive, and poetic life of Canada.

(Harper's 1883, 387)

French-speaking Canada was well on its way to being viewed by Americans as a sort of postcard destination where one could step back into the past, outside the stream of modern American life (see, e.g., Little 2012).

The same was not true of English-speaking Canada. The fact that the population in Upper Canada (what would become Ontario) and in the Maritime colonies was predominantly English-speaking and protestant, and that a significant share of Upper Canada's population traced its ancestry to the United States, even after the wave of British immigration that began following the War of 1812, established a cultural affinity with the American people that did not exist with French Canadians. It is perhaps not surprising, therefore, that there is less that is written in the American press during the 19th century about the character, manners, and behavior of the English Canadian people than about *les canadiens*.

Nevertheless, there are indications that the English Canadian people was seen to be rather different from that of the United States. Alan Taylor cites the accounts of early 19th-century American travelers to Upper Canada who found that those on the Canadian side of the border tended to be less ambitious and not as commercially driven as their American neighbors. This was despite the fact that most of those with whom they spoke in Upper Canada had emigrated from the United States. "In the States," wrote Benjamin Mortimer, a Moravian pastor from Pennsylvania,

> the principal subject of conversation in most public companies which we entered, was the quality of lands. From Tioga to Buffaloe every traveller is supposed to be in quest of them; and little else is cared about, if bargains of that kind can only be made or disposed of to advantage. In Canada, the settlers are more humble in their views. They are mostly poor people, who are chiefly concerned to manage, in the best manner, the farms which have been given them by government.
> *(Mortimer et al. 1954, 25)*

Mortimer added, "What has invited people into Canada, is the free gift of 200 acres, which is made by government to every actual settler" (Mortimer et al. 1954, 25). Such views anticipate an American image of Canadians that would resurface in the 20th century and that, indeed, has long been held by many Canadians in comparing themselves to Americans. It is an image of a people that is more deferential to authority, including that of the state, less ambitious and industrious, and less restless, as Tocqueville uses this latter term, signifying a widespread inability to be satisfied with one's lot, but to "be forever brooding over advantages they do not possess" (Tocqueville 1835, Book 1, Chapter XIII).

At the same time, however, affinities of ancestry, language, and religion, and the fact that the experience of clearing trees in Ohio in order to plant crops was not different from that in Upper Canada, caused Americans to see their neighbors as very much like them, but with an important difference. The neighbors continued to live under the tyranny of British rule. They were oppressed, but surely they longed for freedom!

Thus, it was that the 1837–38 rebellion in Upper Canada, led by William Lyon Mackenzie, tended to be seen by Americans as rather analogous to their own revolution against British tyranny. This interpretation appeared plausible in view of Mackenzie's professed admiration for American institutions and the frequent references to the American revolution in the tracts, editorials, and other publications produced by Mackenzie and other reformers who wished to see an end to British rule in Upper Canada. In "The Declaration of the Reformers of the City of Toronto to their Fellow Reformers in Upper Canada," Mackenzie and his fellow reformers deliberately used language designed to draw an analogy between their cause and that which had motivated America's revolutionary generation:

> The time has arrived, after nearly half a century's forbearance under increasing and aggravated misrule, when the duty we owe our country and posterity requires from us the assertion of our rights and the redress of our wrongs.
>
> The right was conceded to the present United States at the close of a successful revolution, to form a constitution for themselves; and the loyalties with their descendants and others, now peopling this portion of America, are entitled to the same liberty without the shedding of blood – more they do not ask; less they ought not to have. But, while the revolution of the former has been rewarded with a consecutive prosperity, unexampled in the history of the world, the loyal valor of the latter alone remains amidst the blight of misgovernment to tell them what they might have been as the not less valiant sons of American Independence.
>
> *(MacKenzie 1837)*

American support for the rebel cause even took the form of a handful of armed forays into Lower and Upper Canada by American volunteers known as the Patriot Hunters. An estimated 40,000–60,000 members of Hunter Lodges – some estimates place the number much higher – mainly in New York, Ohio, and Vermont, had taken an oath that involved liberating Canada from British tyranny (Buckner 2020, 112–113). Relatively few of them took up arms to invade Canada, and those incursions that took place were unsuccessful. Nevertheless, it appears that the movement had considerable support in the states bordering Lower and Upper Canada (Dagenais 2017). Phillip Buckner argues that their motives and actions need to be understood in the broader context of the sense of Manifest Destiny that was building in the United States, a vision of America's destiny in which there was no place for either Old World powers or non-republic forms of governance on North American territory (Buckner 2020, 113).

Canada as a Refuge From Injustice

The middle of the 19th century saw a new and important image of Canada emerge in the United States. It was, at least in the eyes of some Americans, of Canada as a place of refuge and justice, a promised land for the oppressed. Indeed, one of the refugee slave songs that signaled an intention to escape to Canada was

"O Canaan," Canaan being the biblical promised land. Slavery had been abolished in the colonies of Great Britain in 1834.[6] An estimated 30–40 thousand American slaves escaped to Canada along what became known as the "Underground Railroad," about half of them during the period between the passage by Congress of the Refugee Slave Act in 1850 and President Lincoln's Emancipation Proclamation in 1863.

The image of Canada as a place of freedom for those suffering injustice was popularized by Harriet Beecher Stowe's *Uncle Tom's Cabin*. Published in 1852, it was the best-selling novel in the United States during the 19th century, having an immediate impact on public opinion in the North.[7] Within weeks of its publication, a Boston newspaper declared that "everybody has read it, is reading, or is about to read it" (cited in Brock 2018). In the following passage from the book, fleeing slaves George and Eliza are at a Quaker safe house along the Underground Railroad, heading north to Canada. They have just been talking about what their life will be like when they reach their destination: "But yet we are not quite out of danger," said Eliza; "we are not yet in Canada." "True," said George, "but it seems as if I smelt the free air, and it makes me strong" (Stowe 1852, Chapter XVII, "The Freeman's Defence").

The idea that Canada might be seen as a place of refuge from injustice in America, and where at least some could experience greater freedom than was possible in the United States, was a novel one for Americans. It would resurface during the 1960s and 1970s when an estimated 40,000 American males emigrated to Canada in order to avoid military service during the Vietnam War. In both cases, Canada as the promised land for refugee slaves and Canada as a refuge from service in a war that millions of Americans believed to be imperialistic, Canada's northern neighbor was viewed through the lens of America's internal political and social divisions. And in both cases, the idea of Canada as a place of refuge divided American opinion. Majority opinion in the north and abolitionists across the United States admired Canada's role as a safe haven for fleeing slaves. Southerners rejected the portrayal of slavery presented in Stowe's best-selling book and saw nothing admirable in what they viewed as Canada's complicity in a system that undermined their property rights (Hepburn 1999, 112–114). This was no minor matter. As Benjamin Drew, the author of *The Refugee: Or the Narratives of Fugitive Slaves in Canada Related by Themselves*, wrote, "The escape of slaves forms the most irritating subject of discussion between the North and the South" (Drew 1856, 2). A century later, Canada's reception of what some Americans called "draft dodgers" and others called "war resisters" would again be viewed through the prism of a sharply divided country, although it should be acknowledged that the US government never made a formal issue of Canada's willingness to accept those who evaded the draft or deserted the military.

The image of Canada as a refuge from injustice and worse reemerges in Margaret Atwood's 1985 book, *The Handmaid's Tale*, whose film adaptation by the streaming service Hulu enjoyed great popularity in the American market. Indeed, in the spring of 2021, during the series' fourth season, it was the most popular streaming series in the United States (Hersko 2021). Atwood is a Canadian author. Her nationality and status as a foremost Canadian critic of the United States aside, what is significant here is the resonance that her image of Canada as a place of refuge achieves with Americans. The Underground Femaleroad in *The Handmaid's Tale* evokes the Underground Railroad in the American abolitionist literature of the 19th century, and the dramatic escape of the female protagonist with her child, crossing a river to freedom, is very clearly modeled after Eliza's escape with her child in *Uncle Tom's Cabin*. This image of Canada, and of an important difference between Canada and the United States, is one that has long been shared by significant numbers of Canadians and Americans.

Reciprocity and Annexation

By the middle of the 19th century, Canada was well on the way to being relegated to the margins of the American imagination. The Oregon Treaty established the 49th parallel as the boundary between the United States and Canada in the west, removing what had been the last serious threat that Britain represented to American westward expansion. Although officially neutral during the American Civil War, Britain was perceived by the Union government as a "hostile neutral" (Gambino 2011, interview with Amanda Foreman), providing various forms of support for the Confederacy and having a ruling class that was predominantly supportive of secession by the South. This prompted calls for the annexation of Canada, most significantly a bill entitled, "An act for the admission of the states of Nova Scotia, New Brunswick, Canada East, and Canada West, and for the organization of the territories of Selkirk, Saskatchewan, and Columbia," introduced in the House of Representatives in 1866. Although the bill never got beyond the committee stage in the congressional legislative process, it appears to have generated considerable attention in the American press. In Canada, it was widely believed that the abrogation of the reciprocity treaty between the British North American colonies and the United States, which had occurred just months earlier, was in fact motivated by the American belief "that they could compel us into a closer political alliance with them" (cited in Blegen 1918, 476).

Two years after the unsuccessful annexation bill, a senate resolution was proposed that called on the American government to negotiate a treaty with Great Britain whereby essentially all the territory north of the 49th parallel and west of the Canadian province of Ontario to the Pacific coast and north the border of Alaska would be acquired by the United States. Despite the fact that the proposal had considerable support from certain American interests and was favored by President Grant, it became clear that popular opinion on the Canadian side of the border was, on balance, opposed to joining the United States. The idea quickly lost whatever serious traction it had, as Americans turned their attention to domestic issues in the following decades of rapid railroad construction, westward expansion, and industrialization that followed the Civil War. Occasional musings on Canada becoming part of the United States reflected merely a sense that in the era of Manifest Destiny, Canada's fate was ultimately to become a group of states under the American flag (Wiman 1889, 665).

As was also true in Canada, the issue of annexation often arose in the conversation on reciprocity between the United States and Canada. In the 1850s, when talk about reciprocity was heard increasingly on both sides of the border, if more often in Canada, it was accompanied in the United States by a sense – by no means shared or looked upon favorably by everyone – that Canada was fated to become part of the United States. "The community of interests and pursuits between our northern states and the provinces," declared an article in the *North American Review*,

> is so entire as to scarcely admit of a line of demarkation-.... There are also strong bonds of political sympathy between the colonists and ourselves – stronger, in fact, than unite them with the mother-country .... The circumstances create a strong fellow-feeling. And it is this fellow-feeling that renders commercial restrictions not only oppressive and vexatious, but easy of evasion, and inoperative in proportion to their rigidity and minuteness.
> *(North American Review 1852, 174–175)*

But a swelling sense of Manifest Destiny and what many Americans perceived to be the essential affinities they shared with those on the other side of what was still a quite porous border were not enough to convince everyone that annexation or even, for that matter, the more limited integration promised by reciprocity with Canada would be a good thing. It is not possible to say with any certainty what the balance was between those in favor and those opposed to greater integration with Canada. Nevertheless, it is clear that there were influential political and economic voices on both sides of the issue. It seems, moreover, that annexationist sentiment was strong enough on both sides of the border by the 1850s that Lord Elgin, the Governor-General of the United Canadas (today's Ontario and Quebec), believed that a reciprocity treaty was needed to avoid the eventual absorption of the colonies into the United States. The result was the Reciprocity Treaty of 1854–66 (Lauck 1904, 496–501).

The rather brief moment of renewed talk of annexation that followed the Civil War has already been discussed. Talk of greater trade integration between the two countries also subsided after the government of Prime Minister John A. Macdonald introduced the National Policy of 1879, whose central plank was a significant increase in protective tariffs against goods imported from the United States. But trade between the countries increased nonetheless, and one of the major consequences of the National Policy was a sharp increase in American direct ownership in the Canadian economy, as businesses leap-frogged the tariff wall by establishing production facilities in Canada. Tariff protectionism also was favored by the United

States in the decades after the Civil War, but the tide would turn toward freer trade and a search for markets abroad by the end of the 19th century. Under President Robert Taft, a new reciprocity treaty was negotiated with Canada and ratified by the US Senate, only to be rejected by Canada when the protectionist Conservative Party won the Canadian election of 1911.

Taft's advocacy of the treaty that was at the center of that Canadian election suggests that he saw the greater economic, and ultimately political integration of the two neighboring countries as an entirely natural development in their relationship. In a message to Congress, Taft repeatedly mentions the affinities between Canada and the United States. Speaking of the character and wages of workers on both sides of the border, he declares, "The difference is not greater than it is between different States of our own country or between different Provinces of the Dominion of Canada." After making the economic case for reciprocity, Taft refers to Americans and Canadians as "kindred peoples," and goes on to say,

> The geographical proximity, the closer relation of blood, common sympathies, and identical moral and social ideas furnish very real and striking reasons why this agreement ought to be viewed from a high plane. . . . [Canada] shares with us common traditions and aspirations.
>
> *(Taft 1911a)*

These might be considered mere expressions of goodwill toward Canada and the Canadian people, the sort of thing that would make its way into an official document guaranteed to be widely read and discussed on both sides of the border. But in a letter that Taft wrote to Theodore Roosevelt at about the same time, he writes that "the amount of Canadian [natural resource] products that we would take would produce a current of business between western Canada and the United States that would make Canada only an adjunct of the United States" (Taft 1911b).

Is this proof that Taft's endgame was in fact the annexation of Canada? Perhaps, but only in the sense that he and many other leading Americans of the late 19th and early 20th centuries assumed that the unopposable trajectory of economic development and history would eventually produce this result. This expectation was expressed by the Speaker of the House of Representatives, Champ Clark, during the 1911 Canadian election campaign: "I look forward to the time when the American flag will fly over every square foot of British North America up to the North Pole. The people of Canada are of our blood and language" (cited in Allan 2009, 18).

By the 1920s, the United States had replaced Great Britain as Canada's leading economic partner, being Canada's largest source of imports by far, Canada's major export market, and "New York [had] replaced London as the centre of Canadian borrowings" (Craven 1938, 56). Political annexation was not needed to accomplish what markets had achieved.

The Friendly Neighbor Next Door

As the United States was assuming its place as a world power during the late 19th and early 20th centuries, Americans spared little thought for their northern neighbor. When they did, it was typically in a spirit of goodwill, as in Ernest Hemingway's 1923 poem, "I Like Canadians" (Hemingway 1926). It was written as one part of a pair of poems, the other being "I Like Americans." The contrasting traits that he ascribes to these two peoples are ones that continue to be typical of American images of Canada and how Canadians differ from Americans. Canadians are portrayed as the less ambitious, quieter, more law-abiding but eminently likeable neighbors (Hemingway even remarks on their ice-skating prowess!).

Quiet, law-abiding, and friendly, though perhaps a bit boring and inhabiting a cold land: these have been central to the American image of Canada and Canadians since the beginnings of film in the United States. Pierre Berton describes the Hollywood image of Canada as northern and snowy (pure), peaceful (all those Mounties!), leavened with the occasional rowdy French-Canadian lumberjack or trapper, or a "half-breed" who would generally be portrayed as untrustworthy and even villainous (Berton 1975). This is an image of Canada that was popularized in Jack London's stories of the Yukon and that probably comes close to capturing the image that many Americans continue to have of their neighbor. The image of outdoor simplicity wedded to a humorous brand of folksy wisdom and north-of-the-border quirkiness, provided the premise for "The Red Green Show" (1991–2006), a Canadian comedy that won a loyal cult following on the PBS network in the United States.

But at least as important as the rather simple tropes and images that Hollywood and the American press used in portraying Canada to American audiences is the fact that Canada was, for the most part and most of the time, simply ignored. This may be seen when searching for editorial cartoons that portray Canada in American newspapers during the late 19th and early 20th centuries. They are rare. When they do appear, it is almost always the case that the image of Canada is refracted through its relationship to Great Britain, an acknowledgment of the fact that when it came to international relations, including those between Canada and the United States, Canada was not its own master until after World War I. Canada as a subject in editorial cartoons and in the American press's coverage of international affairs more generally became even less frequent as the role of the United States in world affairs increased.

This might seem ironic, given that the economic relationship between the United States and Canada grew steadily during these times. In fact, however, the explanation is simple enough. Canada posed no sort of a security threat to the United States. Moreover, the main border issues that had occasionally caused friction between the countries were resolved with the 1903 agreement establishing the boundary between Alaska and British Columbia.[8] The two countries also had agreed to create a bilateral International Joint Commission to help resolve boundary waters issues, heralded by both sides as an unprecedented and exemplary model of international cooperation.

The United States had pressing concerns in Latin America and the Caribbean, in Europe, and in Asia. Canada could be taken for granted, and by and large it was.

When Americans turned their attention to Canada in a serious manner – beyond the tourist guide hackneyed images and tropes that would occasionally make their way into popular magazines – seeking to understand its politics and society and its relations with the United States, it would be through the work of American-based academics whose efforts were supported by the Carnegie Endowment. It financed four conferences on Canadian–American relations held at border locations in the northeast between 1935 and 1941, and a series of 25 books on these relations. As Carl Berger writes, "The whole project was initiated, largely supervised, and partly written by Canadian-born scholars in the United States aided by scholars who were American-trained and living in Canada" (Berger 1972, 36). It is perhaps worth adding that precious little such work was being done at Canadian universities, where Britain's history was still far more likely to be taught than Canada's. "By the mid-1930s," writes Berger, "there were more courses in Canadian history being taught in the United States than in Canada" (Berger 1972, 34).

With few exceptions, the persons involved in the Carnegie project – both the academics and the business persons who were associated with it – believed that the histories and destinies of Canada and the United States were intimately and inextricably intertwined and that greater North American integration was both desirable and inevitable. It is, therefore, more than a little ironic that what would become in Canada the two most influential volumes in the Carnegie series on Canadian–American relations, Harold Innis' *The Cod Fisheries* (1940) and Donald Creighton's *The Commercial Empire of the St. Lawrence* (1937), ran strongly against the grain of this interpretation. This had everything to do with the wave of Canadian nationalism or, to put it more frankly, anti-Americanism that gained momentum in Canada during the 1950s. Thus, at the same time as the Carnegie project marked a major advance in Canadian studies in the United States, it would also sow the seeds of an important division between American academics studying Canada, many of whom were Canadian-born, and some of their Canadian-based colleagues. It would not take long before Canadian nationalists came to see the prevailing interpretation of Canadian–American relations expressed in the Carnegie series as indicative of American intellectual imperialism. The fact that the funding for the Carnegie book series and conferences came from a major American foundation and that the endeavor and its continentalist conclusions were applauded by American business just confirmed the suspicions of Canadian nationalists.

During this period, the US government occupied the role of interested observer. Already in the 1930s, the increasing importance of Canada to the American economy was acknowledged by officials in the State Department (Stewart 1992, 145–9). They advocated greater continental economic integration, a strategy intended to pull Canada away from the British Empire system of preferential tariffs and bring about a recognition of what a former Harvard professor and Canada expert at the State Department referred to as "Canada's natural economic ties . . . with the United States" (Stewart 1992, 146). At the same time, and despite the fact that by 1950

Canada was the United States' major trading partner, its main source of imports for a number of strategically important raw materials, and the main location for American direct foreign investment, the relationship with Canada occupied much less time and energy in American government circles than the bilateral relationship might seem to have warranted. The uncomplicated explanation for this was provided in a 1950 State Department memorandum:

> Perceiving no reason to fear or envy the Canadians, we have the friendliest of feelings towards them as neighbors and as partners in various international endeavors, including the Cold War. We have no designs on their territory or their sovereignty. In fact, *we are not as a rule deeply interested in or well-informed about Canadian affairs* (emphasis added). As for harmonious relations, we are inclined to take these for granted, having too many compelling troubles elsewhere in the world to search for more beneath the surface of U.S.–Canadian relations.
>
> *(quoted in Stewart 1992, 195)*

While there was what might be described as a generally and sometimes even strongly supportive disposition among State Department officials for greater Canada–US economic integration, it would be too much to describe this as an imperialist strategy for domination of America's northern neighbor. Such a strategy was unnecessary when Canadians themselves proved so willing, for so long, to cooperate in this continentalist enterprise. "At every critical stage of the increasingly integrated relationship," writes Gordon Stewart, "Canadian governments led by freely elected, experienced, and well-educated politicians, advised by competent officials, chose to follow the path of cooperation with the United States" (Stewart 1992, 197).

And so it must have come as something of a surprise to American policy-makers when, beginning with the Diefenbaker government (1957–63), Canada showed itself to be quite unwilling to bend to their preferences. This would be evident in matters of trade, the refusal to allow nuclear missiles on Canadian soil under Canada's NORAD commitments, and in Diefenbaker's hesitancy to put the Canadian military on alert during the early days of the Cuban Missile Crisis. Equally perplexing must have been the surge in anti-American Canadian nationalism during years when billions of American investment dollars were providing much of the basis for the growth of the Canadian economy and the increasing prosperity of its citizens.[9]

The period bracketed by the Carnegie project on United States–Canada relations and the sanguine attitude that American policy-makers generally took toward their country's relationship with its northern neighbor during the 1950s was one in which Americans who paid attention to Canada – they were relatively few in number – came to believe in the special relationship between the two countries. This involved more than the expressions of goodwill that were by then rather routine from American presidents and other public officials. Moreover, it was quite different from the annexationist expectations held by some since the mid-19th century. The idea of a special relationship between the United States and Canada was placed on an intellectual footing by the Carnegie Foundation scholars and their

Canada 77

FIGURE 3.3 President Kennedy's speech to the Canadian Parliament on May 17, 1961, is often cited, particularly by Canadians, as a classic expression of the special relationship between the United States and Canada.

Photo in the public domain.

research, whose operating assumption was that the social, cultural, and economic ties between the two countries were of a scale and intimacy that made cooperation and an exceptional degree of integration necessary and mutually beneficial. This sentiment would be famously expressed by President Kennedy in his 1961 speech to the Canadian parliament: "Geography has made us neighbors. History has made us friends. Economics has made us partners. And necessity has made us allies. Those whom nature hath so joined together, let no man put asunder" (Kennedy 1961).

The American business elite, which by this point was quite familiar with Canada as their country's major export and import market, as well as the single largest national destination for American direct investment, agreed with Kennedy's sentiments. A 1954 booklet published by the United States Chamber of Commerce offered this homely analogy:

> Canada is not the same as the United States . . . even as you are not the same as the man next door. For all that you like each other, help each other and get along fine, you each live in your own house, know where your lot line runs and you wouldn't think of removing the boundary marker.
>
> It is enough to say that both families and both nations are the best of friends, have many interests in common and each needs the other.
>
> *(Ericsson 1954, 35)*

The term "special relationship" was reserved by Americans for their relations with the United Kingdom, for reasons having overwhelming to do with security matters. But the idea of a special relationship with Canada that involved unmatched intimacy and commonality of interests was agreed by those American opinion-leaders who paid attention to their neighbor. Indeed, the proof that such a relationship existed, as expressed in the 1950 State Department memorandum quoted from earlier, was that Canada could, by and large, be taken for granted.

The Popular Image of Canada: Public Opinion and the Media

The view that Canada could be taken for granted was shared, at least implicitly, by most Americans. Indeed "view" might be overstating the matter. "Sentiment" or "feeling" might be closer to the mark. Lacking either much interest in or information about Canada, the vast majority of Americans had a positive but unfocused image of the country and its people. Indeed, it appears that pollsters very infrequently asked Americans how they felt about Canada until the 1970s (Sigler and Goresky 1974, 637–638). A 1968 Gallup survey found that 94 percent of respondents gave Canada a favorable rating. This was followed by a 1971 survey, commissioned by the Canadian embassy in Washington, that used the same methodology as Gallup and which found that 93 percent had a favorable image of Canada (Sigler and Goresky 1974, 639). These ratings were higher than for any other country.

With very minor ups and downs, this has remained the case since then. Canada has been the most favorably viewed country almost every year since the late 1980s, when Gallup began to ask this question of respondents in a number of countries on a regular basis.[10] In most years, four or five out of ten American respondents say that they have a very favorable view of Canada and about nine of ten say that they have a very or mostly favorable view (Gallup n.d.).

The rather unfocused image that Americans have long had of Canada may be seen in beliefs about the comparative importance of their country's trade with Canada. A 2002 survey found that only 14 percent of respondents identified Canada as their country's main trading partner. Japan was named by 27 percent and China by 25 percent (Ipsos 2002). At that moment in time, Canada had been the United States' major trading partner by a large margin over any other country for a half-century. Rather ironically, as Canada became more important to the United States as an export and import market, and as a destination for investment, there is no evidence that awareness of its importance kept pace with this change.

This may be seen in American media coverage of Canada. In her study of foreign news coverage in selected newspapers between 1927 and 1997, Cleo Joffrion Allen found that only 9.1 percent of all such articles mentioned Canada, compared to 52.7 percent on Western Europe, 19.7 percent on Asia, 18.3 percent on Eastern Europe, 10.5 percent on Latin America, and 10.2 percent mentioning the Middle East (Allen 2005, 68). Mentions of Canada or of organizations based in Canada actually declined over the period of this study, from 14.4 percent of all foreign news stories in 1927 to 8 percent in 1997 (Allen 2005, 70–73). A 1977 survey article entitled, "Foreign News Coverage in American Media," published in the *Journal of Communication*, manages to avoid any mention whatsoever of media coverage of Canada (Lent 1977). Christopher Belch's study of Canadian coverage in five American newspapers over a two-month period in 2004 concluded that, in addition to the relative scarcity of attention paid to Canada, "the underlying ethos of American media exposure to Canada seem[ed] to be through sports, particularly hockey and auto racing" (Belch 2004, 43). Coverage by the influential and nationally read the *New York Times*, he observes, very much confirmed the liberal view of Canada. "In many ways," Belch writes,

> The *New York Times* portrays Canada as the alternative to the United States. A couple articles seem to suggest that Canada is made of all the good things found in the United States, but is a more tolerant place for those who disagree with American policy to seek a political and philosophical safe haven.
> *(Belch 2004, 51)*[11]

In terms of how Canada and Canadians are portrayed, it is by and large the case that the images and tropes that developed in the 19th century continued throughout the 20th century and still exist today. A *New York Times* collection of almost 25,000 images related to Canada, compiled over roughly a century from the late 1800s to the end of the 1990s, was displayed in Toronto in 2017 (Bergeron 2017). A CBC documentary entitled "Imagining Canada," based on that collection, summarizes it as follows:

> It's a perspective that is familiar, yet different, somehow. It casts us as a vast and expansive nation with clusters of people, carving roads through mountains and floating logs down rivers. But we're also seen as a nation of hockey players, immigrants and Indians. A place where the Royals come to holiday and our brightest stars go south to make it big.
> *(CBC 2019)*

In 1997, the NPR radio program, "This American Life," produced what remained for several years one of its most listened to episodes entitled, "Who's Canadian?" It begins with a conversation in which Americans at dinner together are surprised to hear that such iconic American celebrities as Peter Jennings, the longtime television news anchor at ABC, and William Shatner, of Star Trek fame, are Canadians. "It isn't just that there are Canadians among us," observes the program's host, Ira Glass, "it's that they're at the very epicenter of our culture." But their Canadian origins are not known to Americans, or at least to very few. This is liable to cause a brief moment of surprise and perhaps even disorientation, followed by the conclusion that, after all, Canadians are not really different from Americans, notwithstanding that their country seems a pleasant but rather dull place where nothing very eventful happens. More than most American accounts of what it means to be Canadian and how they are different from Americans, "Who's Canadian?" explores in a thoughtful manner the similarities and differences between them. One comes away with the sense that the differences are pretty minor and that Canadians who want to "make it" leave for the United States. This latter conclusion is one that has long existed among many Canadians.

A rather romantic and even somewhat bucolic image of Canada continues to exist in the American media. A good illustration of this is found in "Nova Scotia, Mon Amour," by *Boston Globe* journalist Alex Beam. Beam waxes nostalgic about a place and pace of life from the past, "a treasure that I would prefer to keep to myself," he says, rather than see overrun by hordes of tourists and the modern attractions and amenities they would doubtless expect (Beam 2006). "There are more people in California than in all of Canada!" announced sports host Al Michaels during a video narrated by NBC news anchor Tom Brokaw at the beginning of the 2010 Winter Olympics in Vancouver. Vast pristine spaces and unspoiled nature that would have warmed the hearts of Theodore Roosevelt and John Muir provided the wallpaper for Brokaw's six-minute introduction to Canada for American television viewers (NBC 2010).

Canada surfaces occasionally in American popular culture. When it does, it is almost always in some way that is at best only marginal to the story or, in some cases, as something comic. The creators of *South Park*, an animated TV sitcom, made the Canadian invasion of the United States the ridiculous premise for their 1999 film, *South Park: Bigger, Longer & Uncut*. Canada also makes an appearance in several of the episodes of this long-running TV series. In one of them, it is discovered that Saddam Hussein has gone into hiding and then surfaces as the prime minister of Canada. A handful of episodes from *The Simpsons* include segments in Canada, including one from 2002 in which Homer asks "Canada? Why should we leave America to visit America Jr.?" *Boston Legal*, *How I Met Your Mother*, and *30 Rock* are among the more recent successful primetime television programs that have included Canadian characters or episodes set in Canada. With the exception of *How I Met Your Mother*, in which Robin Scherbatsky, one of the main characters, is a dual-nationality Canadian journalist living in Manhattan, references to Canada are usually fleeting and involve fairly predictable elements of comedy and irony. Canada is the somewhat quirky, but friendly, northern neighbor.

Canada in America's Culture Wars

Canada also surfaces from time to time as either an exemplar or cautionary tale in America's culture wars. For those toward the liberal end of the political spectrum, Canada has long been a place to be envied and emulated. Actor Martin Sheen, upon being awarded the 2004 Christian Culture Medal by Assumption University in Windsor, Ontario, captured this sentiment: "I feel more human when I cross this border. . . . You are more civilized [than us]" (Assumption University 2004).

A rather similar sentiment was repeated by President Barack Obama in his 2016 address to the Canadian Parliament when he warmed Canadian hearts by saying, "The world needs more Canada" (Obama 2016). Senator Bernie Sanders has regularly pointed to Canada as the model that the United States should follow when it comes to negotiating lower drug prices with pharmaceutical companies. Sanders and many progressive Democrats in the United States have long argued that Canada's single-payer health-care model should be adopted in the United States.

This idea of Canada as a sort of Nirvana North first emerged during the era of the Underground Railroad, leading Black Americans to freedom. It was reinvented in the 1960s. Disillusioned by the Vietnam War and violent race relations, liberal-leaning Americans discovered on their northern border what appeared to be a social democratic refuge, a model of what America could and should be. An illustration of this image of Canada is found in documentarist–activist Michael Moore's film, *Bowling for Columbine*. Moore is shown in Windsor, Ontario, where what he claims to be harmonious race relations are compared to the problems of Detroit across the river, and where a local gun store owner cannot remember when there was gun-related murder in his city. Moore moves on to Toronto, where apparently people feel so safe that no one locks their door and where public housing looks positively splendid. He then visits Sarnia, across from Port Huron, where young Canadians muse on how crazy the world across the border seems. A man released from a hospital is visibly surprised when Moore asks him what his treatment cost; "In Canada," he says, "health care is free!"[12]

The election of Justin Trudeau in 2015 blew fresh air into the sails of this image, producing such northern-envy stories as the *Rolling Stone's* 2017 article, "Justin Trudeau: North Star," (Rodrick 2017), the *New Yorker's* 2017 piece, "We Could Have Been Canada" (Gopnik 2017), and William Kristoff's 2017 article, "Canada, Leading the Free World," in the *New York Times* (Kristoff 2017). As Jennifer Bannister observes regarding what she refers to as the American liberal gaze, "What we [Canadians] enjoy is what America lacks: peaceful evolution, social-democratic commonwealth, and more cultural sanity, social equality, and public rationality." But in the end, she argues, "American liberals' gaze towards Canada may be rose-coloured, but more than anything it's myopic. They just don't seem to see much" (Bannister 2017).

The very positive image of Canada embraced by many liberal opinion-leaders, sometimes bordering on the rhapsodic, has never been shared by their conservative counterparts in the United States. In recent decades, Canada has been criticized by social conservatives for its recognition of same-sex marriage in 2004, more than a decade before the US Supreme Court's ruling on this matter, unwillingness to pull its weight when it comes to defense spending and, in the years following the terrorist attacks of 9/11, lax immigration rules that both Democratic and Republican lawmakers, to say nothing of conservative talk show hosts, believed made the Canada–US border a security problem for the United States (Moens and Gabler 2011,

19; Jones 2004). Canada's health-care system, admired by many American liberals, has long been reviled by conservatives as "socialized medicine" and a model to be avoided (Blackadar 2007). Trevor Harrison offers many examples of what he calls anti-Canadianism – all from the right of the American political spectrum – while acknowledging that it is a "shallow phenomenon," used almost entirely for domestic political purposes and not shared by most Americans (Harrison 2007).

But despite all this, it must be said that, most of the time, for liberals and conservatives alike in the United States, Canada is simply not on the radar screen. Spikes of attention occur when something bad happens, such as the interception in 1999 of the so-called Millennium bomber at the border between Washington and British Columbia, the 2003 discovery of BSE ("mad cow" disease) in Canadian cattle herds, and the shocking revelations in 2021 of unmarked graves containing the bodies of hundreds of Indigenous children who had attended residential schools run by churches and the federal government in the provinces of British Columbia and Saskatchewan. As concern over climate change became more widespread, the Alberta oil sands and the proposed Keystone XL Pipeline, which would have carried much of that province's oil across five states to refineries on the Gulf of Mexico, galvanized enormous opposition among liberals, environmentalists, and Indigenous groups in the United States. Far from being a beacon of progressivism, they saw Canada as a poster child for an outdated and globally irresponsible model of energy generation.

Canada's usual absence from the American radar screen changed in February of 2022. The cause was a convoy of truckers and their supporters, referred to as the "Freedom Convoy," that crossed the country from Vancouver on its way to Ottawa. Their trucks blocked the city's center, across from Parliament Hill, in protest against the Canadian government's measures to limit the spread of the COVID-19 virus. These measures included mandatory vaccination for truckers crossing the US–Canada border. The protesters remained dug in for over three weeks. During this time, the busiest border crossing in North America, connecting Detroit, Michigan, and Windsor, Ontario, and crossed by about 10,000 commercial trucks on an average day, was blocked by protesters on the Canadian side for six days.

American media coverage of these events was extensive and much of it was very favorable, if rather surprised. Ideologically conservative commentators, led by those at Fox News, portrayed the demonstrators as nothing short of heroic, very much in the tradition of the Boston Tea Party. Prime time host Tucker Carlson went so far as to call the Freedom Convey "the single most successful human rights protest in a generation" (quoted in Allsop 2022). Popular podcaster Joe Rogan intoned that Canada was a "country in revolt" (Rogan 2022). When the Canadian government controversially invoked the Emergencies Act to bring the Ottawa protests to an end, former President Trump expressed the disappointment and even anger of the American right:

> The tyranny we have witnessed in Canada in recent weeks should shock and dismay people all over the world. . . . A line has been crossed – you're either

with the peaceful truckers or you are with the left-wing fascists. . . . We stand with the truckers and we stand with the Canadian people in their noble quest to reclaim their freedom.

(quoted in Blatchford 2022)

Other parts of America's media system were less positive in their assessment of what the Canadian protests represented, emphasizing what they argued to be the influence of far-right money and organizers from the United States, and arguing that the protests were infiltrated by fascist and racist elements (Levitz 2022). The headline, "'Freedom Convoy' shows the Americanization of Canada's right," captured rather well this critical narrative of what was really going on in Canada's usually orderly and even rather boring capital city (Coren 2022).

How this story was framed by American commentators almost certainly said more about the deep political and cultural divisions in the United States than it did about Americans' perceptions of Canada and Canadians. At the same time, however, there were important elements of the coverage, on both the right and the left, that were nurtured by long-standing tropes about Canadian society and politics. On the right, and although seldom expressed explicitly, there was a surprise that this remarkable show of opposition to policies that protesters saw as undemocratic limitations on rights and freedoms emerged *in Canada*. One had the sense that if it had occurred in France, with its long history of political protests in the streets and paralyzing the country's transportation system, or just about anywhere in the United States, the conservative media would have been no less supportive, though much less surprised. But that this should happen in Canada, for decades portrayed by the American right as a rather statist, too deferential, and semi-socialist place, seemed to warrant at least mild astonishment.

On the left, the emphasis on what was argued to be the influence of the American far right on the protests was fed by a rather similar trope about Canada, but one that saw virtue where the American right saw vice. The scale and duration of the anti-COVID-19 regulations protests in Canada were, according to this view, entirely out of character with Canadians' core values and more usual political behavior. They could only be explained, therefore, by regrettable outside – that is, American – influence. This moment in Canadian political history was understood by American opinion-leaders, across the ideological spectrum, not only through pre-existing filters about their northern neighbor but also through the filter of their own domestic cultural and political conflicts. Canadians return the favor when they observe and interpret events in the United States.

The truckers' protest story, as has always been true of all stories concerning Canada, turned out to have a rather short shelf-life in the American media system, not least of all because of the Russian invasion of Ukraine later that same month. It was unusual in the scale and intensity of the coverage that it received, if only for a few weeks. More typically, however, stories about Canada may receive coverage in such places as the *New York Times* and the *Washington Post* (often in articles written by Canadian journalists) or on NPR, which like those national newspapers caters to a predominantly liberal and more educated audience. The vast majority of Americans will not read or hear them. The ripples that they send across the American conversation tend to be weak and short-lived, and their impact on the ideas that Americans have about their northern neighbors is barely perceptible.

Conclusion

Vast spaces, a cold climate, with friendly people who are much like us in most ways: this is probably a fair summary of the image that most Americans have of their northern neighbor. It is a rather unfocused image that is based on very little knowledge about Canada. Of course, the same could be said for Americans' image of most countries and their peoples. In the case of Canada, however, this is a country that until recently was perennially the United States' major trading partner and with which Americans share a border of almost 9,000 kilometers. As President Kennedy said, "Geography has made us neighbors. History has made us friends. Economics has made us partners." One might imagine, given the scale and duration of this intimacy, that Canada would occupy a bit more space in the thoughts of Americans.

This was not always the case. Indeed, for several decades after the Revolutionary War, Canada was thought of as a security threat to the United States. This was during a time when Canada was firmly under the control of the British authorities, whose aspirations and presence on the North American continent were seen to be inimical to both the American system of government and the westward expansion of the United States. With Canada's gradual independence from the United Kingdom and the dramatic increase that took place in the 20th century in trade and security linkages between the United States and its northern neighbor, the image of Canada became much more favorable. Ironically, perhaps, this was accompanied by less attention being paid to Canada. It came to be seen as a place that could be taken for granted and about which Americans need not worry. Thus the surprise and puzzlement among American leaders, and the repeated need to explain Canada to Americans, that have often accompanied serious disagreements between these two neighbors (Taylor 2014).

Notes

1 Canada acquired gradually the full set of conditions generally associated with sovereignty, and not completely until 1982.
2 Jefferson, who wrote the Declaration, is said to have read Locke's Second Treatise on Government at least three times. All of the principle thinkers of the Revolutionary Era and those who wrote and argued for the ratification of the US Constitution were disciples of Lockean liberalism.
3 Today we would refer to his role as an ambassador. Livingston was an important figure in the negotiations leading to the Louisiana Purchase.
4 The first United States census of 1790 reported that 1.6 percent of the population was Catholic.

5 The balance of historical interpretation strongly suggests that the rebellion had much more to do with French-Canadian nationalism and restiveness under British domination that it did with a true desire to establish an American-style system of government in Lower Canada.

6 Although slavery continued to be legal in the British North America until 1834, there were very few slaves remaining in the colonies in the years before abolition. The last recorded slave transaction in Upper Canada, where most escaping slaves from the United States sought refuge, was in 1824.

7 Uncle Tom's Cabin first appeared in the abolitionist newspaper, *The National Era*, in 41 weekly installments between June of 1851 and March of 1852.

8 It should perhaps be added that the prevailing sentiment among Canadians in regard to this treaty was one of betrayal by the Mother Country. The British representative voted with the three American representatives on the commission that agreed to this boundary. The two Canadian representatives refused to vote.

9 Although the Canadian left has always vigorously denied that American capital was in any way essential to the economic development of Canada and the growing prosperity of its citizens in the postwar years, this has not been the view of most economists and serious economic historians.

10 Although Americans almost always give Canada their highest favorability rating, polls show that they have often considered the United Kingdom to be their best friend and ally, sometimes by a very wide margin. See, for example, Ipsos (2002).

11 This Canadian difference is not always viewed positively from the liberal side of the American political spectrum. See Kaufman (1983).

12 The picture that Moore paints of Canada, it must be said, is highly selective, inaccurate in some respects, and quite misleading. But that's another story.

4
A STORY OF ASYMMETRY

The Policy Consequences of National Images

Introduction

The impact of national images on politics and policy is occasionally obvious, immediate, and even dramatic. An example of this is the hostage-taking at the American embassy in Tehran in 1979. America's image as the "Great Satan" was very much established in the part of the Iranian population that celebrated the return of Ayatollah Khomeini from exile and the end of the Shah's US-supported regime. Indeed, the roots of this image of America go back to the CIA-engineered coup that ousted Iranian Prime Minister *Mohammad Mosaddegh* from power in 1953. Regardless of whether the storming of the embassy compound and the kidnapping of American citizens were orchestrated by the revolutionary Islamic government – a matter on which there is some disagreement[1] – it was supported by the Islamist elite that had come to power and that had widespread support in the general population.

A rather different example of the immediate and significant impact that a national image can have on opinion and behavior toward a country and its government involves the 2008 election of Barack Obama as president of the United States. With relatively few exceptions, his victory was greeted in countries across the world with sentiments ranging from relief to elation, certainly in most democracies (Remez and Wike). Many Parisians literally danced in the streets during the wee hours of the morning when Obama's election was declared by the American media. There was a widespread sense that what the French call, "l'Amerique qu'on aime" (Boulet-Gercourt 2012) – the America we love – had returned. In the words of the German newspaper, *Bild*, "Everyone has now fallen freshly in love with the new America, the other America, the good America, Obamerica, even" (quoted in Remez and Wike 2008).

The idea of a love affair being renewed, and of the America that we love, arose from the ambivalent image of America that was prevalent for many decades before

DOI: 10.4324/9781032675220-4

Obama, and certainly since the 1960s, if not much earlier. It was an image of a country whose ideals and accomplishments were widely admired. At the same time, however, what were often seen to be its failings were also part of this national image, ready to "emerge from the cellar," as Fält puts it, when triggered by particular events or policies. As is evident in Chapter 2, Canadians have never been strangers to this ambivalence.

More often, however, the influence of national images is subtle, indirect, experienced over time, and quite difficult to isolate from other factors. It operates as a set of stereotypes, sentiments, and premises about the other that provides a structure for interpreting its actions and their consequences. For example, the long-standing belief among Canadians – not all, but probably most over the entire history of Canada–US relations – that Americans tend to be arrogant and boastful when it comes to their country and its institutions, and excessively materialistic when it comes to their personal lives, may predispose Canadians to feel and express a sense of moral superiority to their neighbors and to interpret the choices of Americans and of those who govern them as being motivated by inferior moral values. There is no shortage of evidence that many Canadians have viewed Americans in this manner, from 19th-century characterizations of American democracy as "mobocracy," to the early-mid-20th century belief that "freedom wears a crown," to the contemporary conviction that Canada's welfare state, multiculturalism, and less militaristic foreign policies are proof of this moral superiority. This widespread belief exists in the background, and sometimes in the foreground, of any conversation in Canada on national identity, and often surfaces in discussions of Canada–US relations.

Changes in government, decisions regarding whether to go to war, and exceptionally intense bilateral conflicts are moments when the image held by the general population and elites of one country regarding another may become more evident and impactful than is more typically the case. Over the course of US–Canada relations, such moments have been frequent, and generally from the Canadian side. The asymmetry in this intimate relationship has long been such that issues that have roiled the waters of Canadian politics and even generated national debates about Canada's identity and relations with its great neighbor have been little more than a "cinder in the eye" on the other side of the border (quoted in Stewart, 96).

The asymmetric interdependence of these two neighbors is long-standing and well known. Nevertheless, a reminder of its nature and scale may be helpful in order to establish the background against which mutual images exist, and how they may influence the politics of the US–Canada relationship.

Economics

For most of the period since the end of World War II, the United States and Canada have been each other's major trading partner. In recent years, the gap between Canada and some other countries, notably China and Mexico, as America's main partner has closed. Nevertheless, Canada remains the major supplier of energy to the United States and its main partner in the important automotive and energy sectors. Going back to the late 19th century, but particularly since the middle of the 20th century, many of Canada's leading corporations in the manufacturing and resources sectors have been American subsidiaries. Foreign investment in the non-financial sectors of Canada's economy accounted for about one-third of the value of all assets by the early 1970s, roughly four-fifths of which was American direct investment. Since then, it has fallen to about one-quarter of all non-financial assets, about half of this value being owned by American corporations. Canada is one of the largest foreign investors in the American economy (third, after Japan and the Netherlands, as of 2021), but the total value of this investment has never been more than about 10 percent of total foreign investment in the United States (United States 2022).

From the Canadian side, trade dependence on the United States has been an important fact of life for all of the last century, but particularly since World War II. Over the last several decades, trade with the United States has accounted for roughly 20–30 percent of the country's GDP, and close to twice that share in the case of Ontario, the largest province. During most of this period, including recent years, most of Canada's provinces have traded more with the United States, particularly in terms of exports, than with the rest of Canada. Although Canada has been for decades the single largest trading partner for most American states – about 40 of the states by the end of the 1900s, and still over 30 states today – this trade seldom has accounted for more than 3–5 percent of a state's GDP. Michigan, whose automotive industry is closely integrated with that of Ontario, is the main exception. Nationally, the value of trade with Canada has amounted to only about 3–4 percent of American GDP over the past several decades.

Security and Defense

Since FDR's Kingston Declaration in 1938, the United States and Canada have had an integrated defense relationship that has become closer and institutionalized over time through a number of treaties and organizations for joint decision-making. The appearance of an equal partnership in such defense institutions as the Permanent Joint Board on Defense (1940), the Military Cooperation Committee (1946), and the North American Aerospace Command (NORAD, 1958) is belied by the reality of enormous asymmetry in the partners' respective contributions to this relationship, as well as the influence that each has on security matters on the North American continent and throughout the world. Nestling under the American defense umbrella enables Canada to spend considerably less on defense than the long-established NATO target of 2 percent of GDP and less, perhaps even much less, than Canadian governments would otherwise have felt compelled to spend without the guarantee of American protection.

This is a case of geography as destiny. When it comes to national security matters, the United States does not and cannot view Canada with indifference or as just another ally. It is the country with which the United States shares a border of 5,525 miles; the country over which Soviet bombers would have had to pass on their way to American targets during the Cold War; a country whose immigration policies, fairly or not, became a source of concern for American policy-makers after the attacks of September 11, 2001; and a country whose relations with states unfriendly to American interests will necessarily be viewed with concern in Washington.

This does not add up to a security relationship in which Canada has had to comply always, fully and promptly with the expressed preferences of the United States. Indeed, since Prime Minister Diefenbaker government's hesitancy to put Canada's military forces on alert in response to President Kennedy's request during the Cuban Missile Crisis, and his refusal to permit American nuclear weapons to be placed on Canadian territory, there have been several instances where Canadian policy-makers refused to move in lockstep with requests from the US government. Some scholars of US–Canada relations argue that these cases demonstrate that asymmetry, even on the scale that characterizes the relationship between these two neighbors, does not mean that the dominant party will always prevail when interests and preferences are in conflict (Keohane and Nye 2012, Chapter 7).

Communication and Culture

From the dawn of commercial radio in the 1920s to the present day, Canadians have shown a pronounced preference for American mass culture. By the end of the 1930s, the most popular radio programs in the United States were also the most popular ones in English-speaking Canada. This was facilitated by a common language and the fact that most Canadians lived within radio reception distance of the US–Canada border. But it also reflected shared cultural preferences that the architects of Canadian cultural nationalism thought to be regrettable and against which Canadians needed protection through a state-owned broadcasting system (Peers 1973; MacLennan 2009).

Today, Americans and Canadians (English-speaking Canadians, at least) watch the same series and films on television, streaming services, and in cinemas. As has been true since the early days of Hollywood, the pipeline flows overwhelmingly in one direction, Canadians consuming cultural products made in the United States. Several generations of Canadians have lived in a media system that is mainly American. On the other side of the border, several generations of Americans have seen and heard little that they would recognize as Canadian, notwithstanding that many of their country's most popular celebrities have been Canadians (Kirtz and Beran 2006; This American Life 1997).

This asymmetry lies at the root of Canadian public policies that, for almost a century, have sought to establish what their proponents have believed to be a more appropriate balance between American and Canadian content in Canada's media system. These policies have been influenced by Canadian images of the United States and of American culture, images held mainly by nationalist political and cultural elites. At the same time, and as will be seen later in this chapter, economic interests on both sides of the border also have been at stake. They complicate the picture when it comes to determining the factors that have generated cultural protectionism and the opposition to it.

The One-Way Mirror

Margaret Atwood's metaphor of a one-way mirror emphasizes the asymmetry that is at the heart of US–Canada relations. Canadians, she says, "observe, analyze, ponder, snoop and wonder" about all that happens on the other side of mirror, while American are by and large unaware that they are being observed and do not know much about who is on the other side of the mirror. "Nobody," she writes, "except at welcoming-committee time, pretends this is an equal relationship" (Atwood 1986).

In fact, analysis of US–Canada relations reveals two asymmetries. One involves the frequency and degree to which the image held of the other appears to have been a factor influencing the political conversation and the actions taken by the government of the beholder. In these respects, the image held of the United States by Canadians has been far more influential than the image held of Canada by Americans. It would be too much to say that one searches in vain for much evidence that the Canadian image in the United States has mattered very much, as Atwood's metaphor of the one-way mirror suggests is the case. But the gross asymmetry is undeniable.

The other asymmetry involves the importance of national images held by the general public and by elites. When an image of Canada has had consequences for American politics and policy, it has been that held by elites, and particularly by members of the governing class. Images and opinions held by the general population appear to have been of little consequence.

This is not true of Canada, as one would expect in a country whose national self-image has been for so long and so closely tied to perceptions of its southern neighbor. Both elite images of the United States and those of the general population have had important consequences for domestic and foreign policy. In recent years, some commentators have argued that a growing confidence in their country's values and identity has reduced the influence that images of the United States have in Canadian politics and on government policies (Environics 2022).

The Modern Era in US–Canada Relations

The following analysis of the relationship between images of the other and politics and policy in the United States and Canada focuses on the years since the mid-20th century. There are two reasons for this. First, it was during this time that Canada emerged from the shadow of the British empire, acquiring an image in the eyes of Americans that became increasingly independent of Canada's colonial past and British ties. For Canadians too, this was a moment of transformation in their self-image. The country's significant role in World War II, when Canadian forces were under the command of Canadians, and not under British officers as had been the case during the first three years of World War I, made an important contribution to this new self-image.[2]

It was also seen at the policy level through such measures as the Canadian Citizenship Act, 1947. Before the passage of this law, Canadian citizens were considered subjects of the British empire, a status that was declared in their passports. At the same time as this law was being debated and passed, there was heated debate over a proposal for a new Canadian flag to replace the Union Jack (Royal Union Flag) and an unsuccessful attempt to change the name of Dominion Day, marking the birth of Canada as a more or less self-governing country within the British empire, to Canada Day. These years just after World War II were ones during which English Canada began in a major and steady way to "shed its definition of itself as British and adopted a new stance as a civic nation" (Igartua 2006, 1).

A second reason for focusing on events since the middle of the 20th century is that a quickening in the security and economic integration of the United States and Canada took place during the 1940s and 1950s. American ownership of Canada's rapidly growing manufacturing sector grew from 30 percent in 1926 to 39 percent by 1948 and to 45 percent by 1954 (Statistics Canada 1983). In some manufacturing sectors, notably rubber and automobiles, American ownership was almost 100 percent. American firms controlled about two-thirds of Canada's fledgling oil and natural gas sector by the early 1950s. In the case of mining and smelting, the American presence grew from 32 percent in 1926 to 51 percent by 1951 (ibid.).

The trade relationship between the United States and Canada grew dramatically during these years. In the 1920s and 1930s, the value of Canadian exports to the United States and the United Kingdom was, in an average year, not significantly different. By the end of World War II, it had tilted sharply toward the United States, and, by 1950, the value of exports to the United States was about four times that of exports to the United Kingdom. In the case of imports, the United States already provided a much larger share of total Canadian imports than the United Kingdom in the years before World War II. This gap became increasingly wide during the postwar years. From the American side, in the years leading up to the War, Canada already had become the major market for US exports[3] and was the single largest source of imports. Canada retained this dominant status in the postwar era, during which time foreign trade became increasingly important to American prosperity (see figure 6 in Irwin 2019).

The security relationship between the United States and Canada also became much deeper and institutionalized during these years, with consequences for each country's image of the other. It was an image that was regularly expressed by Canadian prime ministers and American presidents. President Truman's 1947 address to the Canadian parliament captured what Canadians quickly came to think of as their special relationship to the United States. Speaking of Canada's relations with his country, Truman said,

> Perhaps I should say "your foreign relations with the United States." But the word "foreign" seems strangely out of place. Canada and the United States have reached the point where we no longer think of each other as "foreign" countries. We think of each other as friends, as peaceful and cooperative neighbors on a spacious and fruitful continent.
> *(Truman 1947)*

Truman went on to enumerate the various forms and institutions of defense cooperation that had emerged during the War, observing, "The spirit of common purpose and the impressive strength which we marshaled for action on all fronts are the surest safeguard of continental security in the future" (Ibid.).

Such sentiments would become a commonplace of speeches on those occasions when one country's leader visited the capital of the other. Even President Nixon's 1972 speech to the Canadian parliament, in which he famously said, "It is time for us to recognize that we have very separate identities; that we have significant differences; and that nobody's interests are furthered when these realities are obscured" (Nixon 1972), did not challenge the mutual dependence of Canada and the United States when it came to continental defense.

Nixon's Canadian counterpart, Pierre Trudeau, had flirted publicly with the idea of Canada leaving NATO during the early years of his premiership – a decision that would have caused a major breach with the United States – only to be reined in by his own cabinet (Oliver n.d.). In words that sound oddly similar to the views expressed by Donald Trump during his term as president, Trudeau said, "We should be protecting our internal security, defending our three seas, and then considering other possible international commitments. It is not logical or rational to protect that which is not ours" (statement made at a 1968 press conference, quoted in NATO n.d.). This view found significant support in Canadian public opinion. As Dean Oliver writes,

> By 1968, many Canadians believed the risk of Communist aggression in Europe less immediate than the need for improved social programs and economic and cultural protection against foreign, especially American, influence. United States policies in Vietnam appeared to some as further proof that the real antidemocratic force in world politics lay much closer to home.
> *(Oliver, n.d., emphasis added)*

On the whole, however, the defense partnership that was built during and in the years after World War II has not been subject to serious challenges since then. Squabbles have occurred over aspects of that partnership, but the idea of the United States and Canada as countries that, in JFK's words, "History has made allies," has not been challenged in either country except on the margins of the political conversation. Along with the high level of economic integration across the US–Canada

FIGURE 4.1 This United States Postal Services stamp commemorates the 100th anniversary of the Niagara Railway Suspension Bridge, the first bridge joining the United States and Canada. The bridge was seen as a symbol of what would often be called, in the 20th century, the world's longest undefended border.

Courtesy of National Postal Museum, Smithsonian Institution.

border, shared security interests remain a pillar of what many Canadians and their leaders think of as the special relationship between these two neighbors.

In sum, the years after World War II were characterized by increasing economic integration and deepening defense cooperation. *Time* magazine was the best-selling public affairs weekly on both sides of the border, "Gunsmoke," "I Love Lucy," and a clutch of other weekly television programs were awaited equally by both American and Canadian viewers, and differences between the lifestyles of the two peoples were not easily detectable. All of this contributed to a widespread belief that, as President Truman put it, US–Canada relations were not foreign relations, as this latter term was generally understood. Accounts of these postwar years by politicians and diplomats emphasize the exceptional character of what they did not hesitate to call a special relationship, characterized by an expectation that shared interests, common values, and neighborliness would help to iron out any major differences between them.[4]

But even during what might be thought of as the high point of the US–Canada special relationship, there were signs that the image of the other was not entirely positive and that some government policies were being influenced by these negative perceptions. Almost all of this negativity involved the Canadian image of the

United States. Moreover, and although this is impossible to demonstrate with certainty, negative images of America and its influence on the Canadian economy, culture, and national sovereignty were generated mainly by elites whose anti-American views resonated with what would become an increasing share of the Canadian population, and who were able to point to public opinion as evidence that Canadians supported – indeed, demanded! – protectionist measures of various sorts.

To better understand the role that national images have played in the bilateral relationship between the United States and Canada, four issues will be examined. The first two are broader in scope, involving Canadian policies inspired by cultural nationalism and economic nationalism, both of which grew in political influence beginning in the 1950s. The economic nationalism issue centered on American ownership in the Canadian economy and was the main source of conflict between the two national governments from the late 1960s until the early 1980s. The other two issues are more specific. The first is the free trade agreement negotiated between the United States and Canada in the 1980s and that came into effect in January of 1989. The second is the War in Iraq, and Canada's decision not to support the American-led invasion of that country.

Cultural Nationalism in Canada

The Canadian government's first major step toward the creation of a national cultural policy was the Royal Commission on National Development in the Arts, Letters, and Sciences, popularly known as the Massey Commission. The Commission's 1951 report recommended a wide range of government measures intended to promote Canadian culture and to protect it from American influences that crossed so easily the US–Canada border. There is absolutely no evidence that this inquiry into the state of Canadian culture and what might be done to promote it was a response to popular sentiment. In what is generally accepted as the definitive account of the early decades of Canadian broadcasting policy, up to and including the recommendations of the Massey Report, Frank Peers at no point suggests that public demand for more Canadian content on the airwaves of the nation was a driver of policy. Indeed, he acknowledges that while the organizations that made representations to the Massey Commission were overwhelmingly supportive of a more nationalist broadcasting policy, "Canadians were strongly attracted to the entertainment programs from the United States, and their derivative Canadian equivalents" (Peers 1973, 442). Indeed, when an executive for a private sector Canadian television network declared that "what is wrong with American material? If we are ever to have a Canadian culture, it will come as a result of exposure to what is undoubtedly the fastest rising culture in the world today – that of the U.S.A.," he was rebuked by the Commission's chairman for daring to express a sentiment that was so contrary to the elitist and nationalist spirit of the inquiry (Berkowitz 2021, 94). Indeed, Canadians made very clear through their tastes in television viewing, films, and magazines that they liked what came from America. The Massey Commission and Canadian cultural elites, on the contrary, viewed these tastes as regrettable and characterized American popular culture as an invasion that threatened the independence of Canada.

It is important to recognize that Canadian politics in the postwar era, and indeed arguably until the 1980s, was a largely elitist affair that assumed a culture of deference[5] (Lipset 1990; Cairns 1992; Nevitte 1996). This was expressed in a popular ditty composed by B.K. Sandwell on the occasion of Vincent Massey's appointment in 1952 as governor-general of Canada:

Let the Old World, where rank's yet vital,
Part those who have and have not title.
Toronto has no social classes –
Only the Masseys and the masses.
   (Quoted in Skelton Grant 2015,4)

The rise of postwar cultural nationalism in certain elite circles of Canada passed almost entirely unnoticed in the United States. Indeed, it was not until the 1960s, when the Canadian government proposed to end the tax deduction for advertising that was made available to American magazines with Canadian editions, that cultural protectionism north of the border attracted the unwelcome attention of some American business interests and the policy-makers they lobbied. There is no doubt that the American public has been almost entirely unaware of Canadian media policies that, as explained by Canadian Minister of Canadian Heritage, Sheila Copps, during a 1998 House of Commons committee meeting, were needed to protect Canada's cultural identity from a global "monoculture" emanating from the United States (quoted in Stewart 2010, 40). During this same debate, Quebec senator Serge Joyal went so far as to refer to Canadian cultural protectionism as a tantamount to a policy of national defense (cited in Murchison 2008, 237).

The Canadian public, or at least the attentive public, has been aware for decades that there are voices in their country that have argued persistently and passionately that Canadian culture and identity are threatened by what Minister Sheila Copps called the American "monoculture." Relatively few have heard about or understand the split-run magazine issue that, according to John Stewart, a Canadian who worked at the US embassy in Ottawa, was the longest and most bitter dispute that he witnessed during his almost 20 years there (Stewart 2010, 35). Nowhere in Stewart's account of this issue does he point to the views of the Canadian public as a driver of the dispute. Rather, the belligerents were industry stakeholders on both sides of the border, the state officials who took their respective sides, and members of the Canadian cultural elite whose image of the United States and the threat to Canada had long been summed up in Minister Copps' invocation of the nationalist slogan, "the state, or the United States,"[6] and her description of American culture as a predatory "monoculture." In a very careful and historically thorough examination of Canadian cultural protectionism going back to the dawn of the broadcasting era, Heather Murchison concludes that "contemporary Canadian cultural policy is driven by political elites purporting to protect national identity while shaping legislation to promote stakeholder interests" (Murchison 2008, 3). How could it be otherwise, when the media consumption habits of Canadians have always demonstrated very clearly where their preferences lie? (Based on my personal observations, having taught Canadian politics to roughly 15,000 Canadian university students over a period of more than 40 years, few of them are even aware of such policies as Canadian content regulations in broadcasting, various subsidies for Canadian media producers, and the split-run issue in magazine publishing, that have been so dear to the country's cultural elites and nationalist politicians claiming to speak on their behalf. This elite preference for a significant state role in shaping what is offered to Canadians appears to have begun during the earliest days of broadcasting, when the 1929 report of the Royal Commission on Broadcasting claimed to express a public consensus in favor of a publicly owned broadcasting system that did not in fact exist (Gasher 1998). What did exist, however, was an elite preference for the BBC model that had been adopted in the United Kingdom, and a mistrust and disdain for the American model of private ownership in broadcasting.)

Economic Nationalism in Canada

The anti-American sentiments and beliefs of some Canadian elites were on display several years later when another Canadian royal commission was created to study and make recommendations on the Canadian economy. The Report of the Royal Commission on Canada's Economic Prospects, popularly known as the Gordon Commission, declared,

> There is concern that as the position of American capital in the dynamic resource and manufacturing sectors becomes ever more dominant, our economy will inevitably become more and more integrated with that of the United States.... Behind this is the fear that continuing integration might lead to economic domination by the United States and eventually to the loss of our political independence.
>
> *(quoted in Bliss 1987, 509)*

The "concerns" alluded to by the Gordon Commission's report certainly existed in some political circles, on the part of certain journalists, and among nationalist intellectuals. They were not shared by the Canadian public, at least not at that moment in time. On the contrary, a poll conducted in 1957 found that only one in five Canadians believed that their country's way of life was too influenced by the United States. This poll also found that most Canadians not only believed that American investment had been a good thing, they hoped for even more of it (cited in Wiseman 2022, ft.#10 at p. 237).

Although the American public was by and large unaware of the sentiments expressed by the Gordon Commission on the matter of American investment in Canada, and would remain oblivious to these concerns even as they moved toward the center of the Canadian political conversation in the 1960s and 1970s, this was not the case for certain American policy-makers, business people, and academics. Already in the 1950s, there emerged among these groups an awareness that Canadian nationalism and anti-American sentiment were gaining traction, particularly in the political elite and among English-Canadian opinion-leaders. State Department documents on US–Canada relations reveal a sensitivity toward the political ramifications of the American ownership issue in Canada and the development of an image of Canada, or at least of Canadian nationalists, as irrational, wrong on the facts, and insecure in their relationship with the United States.

This image of Canadian nationalism may be seen in the response of American economists to the Gordon Commission and to the rationale for Canadian restrictions on American investment more generally. American economist Simon Kuznets, who would be awarded the Nobel Prize in Economics in 1971, had this to say about the Gordon Commission's forceful recommendation that Canadian business become less dependent on American capital:

> [W]hat specific useful purpose would be achieved by a greater share of Canadian equity holdings in such enterprises? This is not to say that there are no good answers to these questions; the point is rather that none have been given . . . . At the risk of unwarranted speculation, one might suggest that greater economic "dependence" of Canada upon the United States, a neighbor over ten times its size, whose political decisions and cultural patterns may often not be to the taste of the Canadian community, despite obvious economic gains, involves some psychological costs. The relevant factors are cultural, socio-psychological, and political, rather than economic.
>
> *(Kuznets 1959, 379)*

Harvard economist Richard Caves went further in his skepticism about the Gordon Commission's economic nationalism:

> The Canadians most grieved over enslavement by American Big Business can be found within a stone's throw of Toronto's equivalent of Wall Street. And few Canadian newspapers print more hard breathing prose damning American domination than the *Financial Post*, a weekly oracle of Canadian business and finance. By contrast, the general public in the Canadian cities most completely dominated by subsidiaries of American firms feels at ease with the great southern neighbor except for the standard view that Americans do not know enough about Canada.
>
> *(Caves 1960)*

Even before the Gordon Commission attracted the concern of American economists to what seemed to them to be the gathering strength of irrational fears in Canada, some policy-makers in Washington were aware that nationalist sentiment of irrational fears was complicating their country's relationship with Canada. This may be seen in the following observations from declassified correspondence. The first is from a 1953 memorandum from Secretary of State John Foster Dulles to President Eisenhower, prior to the President's state visit to Canada:

> The Prime Minister will seek an exchange of views regarding *foreign policy and defense*. . . . The defense of North America will probably be discussed, with an estimate of the *threat of Air Attack from the North*, and need for radar installations. For political reasons the Prime Minister does not relish a large build-up of U.S. installations in Canada, will want Canadians to do more in defense of Canada, and will be worried about costs. You could *reassure him of our respect for Canadian sovereignty* and the fact that our mutual defense arrangements are always jointly agreed.
> *(Office of the Historian 1953, emphasis in original)*

This awareness of and sensitivity toward the Canadian government's increasing need to respond to and even placate nationalist views is also seen in a 1954 memorandum sent by the American Chargé d'Affaires in Ottawa to the State Department. The subject was negotiations between the United States and Canada on the construction of the St. Lawrence Seaway:

> [Canadian Minister of External Affairs] Pearson expressed the intention of his group: "We do want to participate in the international section. It puts us in a better position to meet public opinion for a through-Canadian seaway . . . and indeed to build for that all-Canadian seaway of the future" [Canadian Minister of Trade and Commerce]. Howe, later on, was even more explicit, "We have come to the conclusion that this is what we can get away with politically."
> *(Office of the Historian 1954)*

Awareness among American diplomats and State Department officials of the growing political strength of Canadian nationalism is expressed more forcefully in a 1957 memorandum sent from the US Embassy in Ottawa to the State Department:

> Notwithstanding the basic soundness of present Canadian-United States relations, there is in this rapidly developing nation a growing consciousness of national destiny. As the population, industrial base and wealth of Canada increase, so will also the nationalism and sensitivities of its Government and people. The United States must be constantly attentive to this development and, in its own self-interest, continue to exercise the greatest consideration in all aspects of its relations with this country. While there are at present no Government objections

or general local resentments with respect to United States defense activities in Canada, both the Embassy and United States military commanders in this country are constantly on the alert to initiate actions or measures designed to forestall local irritations or criticism. Pursuant to these efforts the United States has, for example, during the past year taken the initiative in an agreement to fly the Canadian flag alongside the United States flag at all United States military installations in Canada, thus forestalling virtually certain criticism from elements seeking instances of United States disregard for Canadian sovereignty.

(Office of the Historian 1957a)

In a memorandum sent on the eve of the 1957 Canadian election by the US Ambassador to Canada, Livingston Merchant, to the State Department, the Ambassador had this prediction:

Although premature [to] predict full implications Canadian election results for Canadian-US economic relationships, Embassy considers that irrespective [of] political alignments there will be gradual veering away from traditional liberal trade policies and intensification of nationalistic feeling with following practical results.

(Office of the Historian 1957b)

Livingstone went on to list seven of these results, all of which involved Canadian government policies intended to reduce Canada's economic dependence on the United States and, possibly, increase economic ties with the United Kingdom and the Commonwealth.

Livingston's prediction that there would be a "veering away from traditional liberal trade policies and intensification of nationalistic feeling" was borne out not only during the Conservative government of John Diefenbaker (1957–62), but for the next two decades. The image of a Canada that could be taken for granted in matters of trade and investment was gone, replaced by one of a rather prickly, insecure, and sometimes uncooperative neighbor. The return to power of the Liberal Party in the Canadian election of 1963 was received with some relief in official Washington, but with a realization that viewing Canada as a sort of northern extension of the United States was no longer possible. In a telegram sent to the State Department by the US Ambassador to Canada a week after the Liberals' victory, William Butterworth wrote:

a somewhat more mature Canada has emerged from the electoral crucible and a measure of its neuroses has been exorcised. . . . I do hope that in future we will deal with Canada with considered care and courtesy but in a more normal, matter-of-fact manner, and with due regard to the importance of obtaining quids for quos.

(Office of the Historian 1963a)

Days later, National Security Advisor, McGeorge Bundy, echoed the Ambassador's belief that Canada's change in government was reason for optimism. In a memorandum to department secretaries that emphasized the special relationship between Canada and the United States, Bundy wrote:

> The advent of a new government in Canada has naturally stirred nearly all branches of the government to new hope that progress can be made in effective negotiations with this most important neighbor on all sorts of problems. It is the President's wish that these negotiations should be most carefully coordinated under his personal direction through the Department of State.
>
> *(Office of the Historian 1963b)*

In the event, Livingston's prediction that regardless of what party formed the government in Ottawa, Canadian nationalism would continue to be an irritant in the bilateral relationship, proved to be true. Just months after the Liberals' return to power, the Canadian government's first budget caused major consternation in the American business community and in Washington. In a memo from Secretary of State George Ball to the US Embassy in Ottawa, Ball referred to the budget as being unfair to American investors and "discriminatory," that it might encourage other countries to pursue similarly discriminatory policies against American investment and foreign investment more generally, that it "erect[ed] new barriers between Canada & US in area where none previously extant," and that all of this was especially surprising coming from Canada, given the closeness of the relationship between the two countries (Office of the Historian 1963c). The most controversial of the measures in the 1963 budget, a tax on foreign takeovers of Canadian firms, was subsequently withdrawn and the political fortunes of Walter Gordon, the unapologetically nationalist finance minister who introduced it, declined rather dramatically.

Economic nationalism in Canada, however, continued to gain traction. The Canadian public, which until the mid-1950s had shown little concern about American investment in Canada, was exposed to a constant and heavy dose of media stories and politicians' claims about what was argued to be the harmful effects that this and Canada's trade dependence on the United States had on their country's economic prosperity and political sovereignty. It was hardly surprising, indeed probably inevitable, that an increasing share of the public would accept the image of the United States as a threat that needed to be resisted through protectionist policies. There followed a steady flow of such policies, particularly during the premiership of Pierre Trudeau. They included his government's 1972 "Third Option" goal of shifting Canadian trade toward the Pacific Rim economies and Europe, the screening of foreign acquisitions of Canadian firms that began in 1974, and the passage of the National Energy Program in 1981, which in the eyes of American investors in Canada's oil and gas sector and policy-makers in Washington, sought to "Canadianize the energy sector" – words used by US Ambassador Paul Robinson at the time (Cohen 1983) – at the expense of American economic interests.

As all of this was happening, the American public was almost entirely unaware of what Ambassador Robinson called a "gathering storm" in US–Canada relations (quoted in Cohen 1983). No surveys were done by Gallup or any American polling organization on any of the issues associated with policies inspired by Canadian nationalism during this period from the 1950s to the early 1980s. There were, however, occasional Gallup polls asking Americans how well they liked foreign nations on a ten-point scale. In 1968 and 1971, years when Canadian nationalism was cresting and Canadians' respect for the United States was decreasing, well over 90 percent of Americans expressed a favorable image of Canada, higher than for the United Kingdom, the second most favorably viewed country. Indeed, the percentage of Americans expressing a "highly favorable" view of Canada in the 1971 poll was 65 percent, compared to 44 percent for the United Kingdom (Sigler and Goresky 1974). More systematic polling of how favorable Americans felt about other countries began in the late 1980s, with respondents being asked whether their opinion of particular nations was *"very favorable, mostly favorable, mostly unfavorable, or very unfavorable."* Gallup began to ask this question about Canada in 1987. There is no reason to believe, either from the earlier polls or from those that began in 1987, that the irritation that Canadian nationalism provoked among some American policy-makers and among those in the business community affected by what were seen as anti-American policies spilled over to influence the American public's image of Canada.

The issue of American investment in Canada, which was so important in the 1960s and 1970s to the Canadian nationalist image of the United States, and that was a key driver of the economic protectionist policies implemented during those years, now appears to be a historical footnote in the relations between the two countries. When Canadians are asked whether foreign investment poses a threat of some sort to their country and its economy, they are more likely to think of China than of the United States. This is despite the fact that American investment continues to account for about half of all foreign investment in Canada, a figure much higher than any other country's share (Statistics Canada 2022). A 2017 poll found that American investment was seen to be no greater a threat across a spectrum of economic sectors than investment from the EU or the United Kingdom, but that attitudes were much less favorable toward Chinese and Russian ownership in the Canadian economy (Angus Reid Institute 2017). This was confirmed in a 2019 survey asking Canadians about investment in high technology sectors (Asia-Pacific Foundation of Canada 2019). Once central to the Canadian image of the United States as a danger to an independent Canada, American ownership has receded to the margins of public consciousness.[7]

United States–Canada Free Trade

In view of the fact that issues of trade, and particularly proposals for free trade, have often been contentious in American politics, one might have expected that the negotiations, signing, and passage by the US government of the Canada–US Free

Trade Agreement in 1988 would have captured the attention of some Americans. It did, but as is always the case, the general public appears to have been unaware and indifferent. There was quite a lot of coverage in the elite press, particularly in the *New York Times* and the *Wall Street Journal*, most of which was favorable. There was also recognition in these media outlets that Canadian opinion on the agreement was sharply divided and that the 1988 Canadian election was fought principally on the issue of free trade with the United States. But unlike in Canada, where there was extensive polling on Canadians' views regarding free trade with the United States, there were no such surveys of American opinion. What we do know is that the law authorizing the agreement passed by a bipartisan vote of 366 to 40 in the House of Representatives and 83 to 9 in the Senate. In view of such overwhelming support from the people's representatives, Gallup and other polling firms presumably saw little reason to ask Americans their views on the matter. In the only poll of American opinion on the Canada–US Free Trade Agreement that I have been able to find, taken two years after the treaty came into effect, elites in the Detroit–Windsor region, the location of the busiest border crossing in North America and an extensively integrated automotive sector, were asked their views. Support for the agreement was overwhelming on the American side of the border at 84 percent. Large bipartisan majorities expressed the view that the agreement would not jeopardize Canadian social programs or make Canada just like the United States (Strate and Sellars 1993).

A majority of the Canadians interviewed in this survey of local elites – about six in ten – supported the free trade agreement. Those who did not believed that Canadian jobs, social programs, and cultural distinctiveness were threatened. These fears were shared by a significant portion of the Canadian population and were expressed before and during the 1988 federal election by spokespersons for the Liberal and New Democratic parties, the country's major unions, some business interests for whom exports to the United States were not important or that felt threatened by the prospect of any lowering of protectionist barriers, and by nationalist cultural elites in English-speaking Canada.[8]

Indeed, the 1980s debate in Canada over free trade with the United States, culminating in the 1988 election, is often pointed to as an illustration of how Canadian images of the United States have affected Canadian policy. As Lawrence Leduc notes, the 1988 election has frequently been described in Canada as a "referendum on free trade." He argues, however, that this is something of a mischaracterization, rightly noting that "a contest between three or more political parties for parliamentary seats can never really be a referendum on any single issue, even one as important as the Canada-US Free Trade Agreement" (Leduc 1989, 167).

This is true, in a strictly formal sense. But it is also true, and even more to the point, that the 1988 campaign was overwhelmingly about free trade with the United States. On no other issue were Canadian voters polled repeatedly during the campaign and in the months leading up to it. Indeed, polling on free trade with the United States began after the 1984 report of the Royal *Commission* on the

Economic Union and Development Prospects for *Canada* (popularly known as the Macdonald Commission) recommended that Canada pursue a free trade agreement with the United States.[9] Polling on the issue, and the free trade conversation more generally, intensified after the Canadian government of Brian Mulroney proposed negotiations on such an agreement to President Reagan in September of 1985. During the 1988 election campaign, almost every household in the country received campaign literature on the issue at their doorstep, much of it from advocacy groups. It dominated the campaign conversation as no single issue had since the 1911 federal election, when the proposal for freer trade with the United States was almost certainly the key factor contributing to the defeat of the Liberal Party. An important part of the anti-free trade messaging to the Canadian public in 1988 relied on political cartoons. Many, indeed, most of these images evoked long-standing tropes and insecurities about Canada being invaded by the United States, economically, culturally, and politically.[10]

Since the late 19th century, the conversation in Canada about free trade with the United States had always been accompanied, and sometimes even dominated, by fears that it would lead to the end of Canada as an independent country. In fact, and until the emergence of a left-wing nationalist critique of US–Canada economic integration in the 1960s, these fears had been stoked by Canadian economic interests that feared competition with American businesses in the domestic market, and by anglophile sentiments that preferred to see Canada in the economic orbit of the British empire (sentiments that were entirely atavistic by the middle of the 20th century). As discussed in Chapter 3, the image of Uncle Sam as having designs on Canadian resources and markets – an image that was often communicated in a sexually suggestive manner (Nielson 2016) – was familiar to the point of banal in Canada, even if not all Canadians believed or worried about it.

It is striking, therefore, that these fears appeared to subside quite dramatically in the mid-1980s, when surveys showed that a clear majority of Canadians supported Canada–US free trade. An Environics poll conducted in April of 1984 found that 78 percent of Canadians were supportive, a figure that dropped to 57 percent two years later when negotiations between the two governments began (Environics 1986). The older image of America as a danger to Canadian independence appeared to have weakened, but it quickly reasserted itself leading up to and during the 1988 Canadian election and the implementation of the Canada–US Free Trade Agreement. When the election was called, support for free trade with the United States stood at only 38 percent, with 42 percent opposed. By the end of the five-week campaign, support had reached 49 percent and opposition had fallen to 36 percent (Colleto 2022). With the passage of time, and rather compelling evidence that the dire predictions of Canadian nationalist voices have not materialized, clear majorities of the Canadian population have supported free trade with the United States for the past 30 years. This does not mean that the image of America as a threat to Canadian independence has lost all traction in Canadian politics and society. It is kept alive at the margins of the political conversation by the Council of Canadians,

104 A Story of Asymmetry

FIGURE 4.2   The personal relationship between President Ronald Reagan and Prime Minister Brian Mulroney was closer than between any other American and Canadian leaders. The free trade agreement agreed by their governments was by far the most contentious issue during the leaders' debates that preceded the 1988 Canadian election. It did not make an appearance in the presidential debates that preceded the 1988 American elections.

Courtesy of Canadian Press, reproduced with permission.

the successor organization to the Committee for an Independent Canada, and by some anti-globalization voices in the New Democratic Party and in academe.

The War in Iraq

More than two decades after the American-led invasion of Iraq, it is widely believed in Canada that public opinion was a major factor in the Canadian government's decision not to participate in the invasion or to endorse it. Moreover, and relatedly, it is also widely believed that the image many Canadians held of the United States as a danger to world peace contributed to Canadian opposition to the war. *Maclean's* 19th annual end of year survey found, in the words of pollster Allan Gregg, "solid sentiment that the United States is acting like a bully," and that "[the American] view of the world is increasingly different from ours" (Gregg 2002, 34). An Ipsos poll taken six months before the March 2003 invasion of Iraq found that a small majority of Canadians agreed that Saddam Hussein and President George W. Bush were equally to blame for what appeared to be imminent war. This survey also found that about four in ten Canadians agreed that the real reason for war was to remove Saddam Hussein from power, even though his regime no longer posed a real danger to world peace (Ipsos 2002).

The Canadian public, and the country's elites, were not of one mind when it came to the American-led invasion of Iraq. The Ipsos poll mentioned earlier found that about four in ten Canadians supported the idea of sending troops to support the removal from power of Saddam Hussein. Moreover, on the eve of the invasion Canada's two most influential English-language newspapers, the *Globe and Mail* and the *National Post* published editorials critical of the Canadian government for its refusal to support the United States. Several of the country's most prominent journalists also supported the use of military force, as did Michael Ignatieff, a well-known public intellectual who was teaching at Harvard at the time and who would become leader of Canada's Liberal Party several years later. The Conservative Party of Canada, under the leadership of Stephen Harper, and the conservative premier of Alberta, Ralph Klein, also supported the American position. Perhaps the voice that resonated most significantly with Canadians who supported the invasion of Iraq was that of Don Cherry, a commentator for "Hockey Night in Canada." His on-air tirade against the Canadian government's refusal to support the United States became an immediate and much publicized lightning rod for anti- and pro-American sentiments.[11]

Divided public opinion, added to the fact that some political leaders and prominent opinion-leaders were strongly in support of formal government support for the invasion of Iraq and even Canadian military engagement, meant that the Liberal government of Jean Chretien had some room to maneuver. Moreover, only four years earlier this same government had shown its willingness to support the NATO bombing of Yugoslavia. This was despite the fact that the action was not approved by the Security Council of the United Nations, which was widely thought of as a necessary condition for Canadian military engagement abroad. Indeed, not only was Canadian public opinion strongly on the side of Canada's military participation in the 1999 NATO mission – a mission that was characterized by anti-American critics in Europe and North America as motivated by the desire to establish American hegemony in the last part of eastern Europe to hold out against such domination – but also every party in Canada's parliament supported Canadian military engagement. Crucially, public opinion in Quebec was in agreement. "Opinion in Quebec has always had a crucial influence on the posture of Canada's foreign relations," writes Michael Manulak. "In sensing the mood in Quebec," he continues, "the government concluded that there was support for Canadian involvement in the Kosovo question" (Manulak 2011, 48).

Granted that Serbia in 1999 and Iraq in 2003 were quite different issues in the eyes of most Canadians. The first was framed by most Canadian opinion-leaders and thought of by most Canadians as a humanitarian intervention, necessary to staunch the genocidal actions of a Serbian dictator, and assessed against the backdrop of the siege of Sarajevo and ethnic cleansing in Bosnia. The second case was framed and thought of in a more complex manner that included narratives regarding the Bush administration's War on Terror, which pointed to the Saddam Hussein regime as a foremost sponsor of international terrorism, the claim that Iraq had or was attempting to develop nuclear weapons, and a widespread belief in much of the West that the underlying motivation had to do with control over oil supply from the Middle East. All of these reasons for invading Iraq were believed by significant shares of the Canadian population to be the principal motivation behind American advocacy of military action (Burkholder 2003).

Crucially, however, public opinion in Quebec was quite different from in the rest of Canada. On the eve of the invasion of Iraq, an Environics poll found that whereas only 27 percent opposed military intervention sanctioned by the United Nations, the figure was 56 percent in Quebec (cited in Policy Options 2003). Every poll taken in the year before the invasion of Iraq showed that public support for military invention, whether with or without UN sanction, was much lower in Quebec than in the rest of Canada. Politically, this mattered. The Liberal government's majority in parliament depended on winning a large number of seats from Quebec. The Liberal Party held 36 of Quebec's 75 seats, with a federal election expected to take place within a year. A loss of just 4–5 percent of the popular vote in Quebec to the Bloc Québécois, the Liberal Party's main rival in that province, would have made it impossible to form another majority Liberal government. There was absolutely no support in the government's Quebec caucus for Canadian endorsement of the imminent war in Iraq. In addition, Prime Minister Jean Chrétien, a Quebecker, was personally skeptical of American motives. Indeed, as he makes clear in his memoir, where he recounts an exchange with British Prime Minister Tony Blair, Chrétien was among those who believed that control over oil was at the top of the list of the Bush administration's motives (Chrétien 2018, 11).

The influence of public opinion in Quebec was magnified by Canada's political party and electoral systems. In no national election over the course of Canadian history has the Liberal Party been able to form either a minority government or a majority government without significant support from Quebec voters. The fact that Quebeckers, much more than other Canadians, opposed the invasion of Iraq is generally explained by stronger anti-militarism sentiment in that province. The roots of this, and whether this sentiment has been fueled by anti-Americanism in recent decades, has been the subject of much debate (see Massie and Haglund 2011; Haglund and Massie 2016). An explanation that involves Quebeckers' image of the other is provided by Jean-Sébastien Rioux: "Quebecers have . . . long perceived that the Canadian military is at the mercy of foreigners who don't have Canadian national interests at heart" (Rioux 2005, 9). In the Boer War and World Wars I and II, those "foreigners" were the British, whose influence in English Canada was seen by French-speaking Canadians to be too strong. In the case of the wars in Afghanistan[12] and Iraq, the "foreigners" were the Americans. In all of these cases, Quebeckers were less supportive of Canadian military engagement than were Canadians in the rest of the country.

On the other side of the border, there is very little evidence that Canada's failure to support the American-led War in Iraq registered with the American public, either evoking existing images about Canada and Canadians, or changing those images in any way. In the months after the American-led invasion of Iraq, CBC television news featured a story in which one of its reporters drove around the north of Ohio, within close driving distance of Canada, and asked residents of the state about Canada's position on the war. None of the interviewees had any idea that not only was Canada not a part of the Anglo-American coalition but that most Canadians were opposed to the war. Although by no means a scientific sample of the American population, it seems likely that most Americans did not share the disappointment and pique of their ambassador to Canada, who described the Canadian government's decision as tantamount to one family member letting down another.[13] Favorable sentiment toward Canada remained at about 90 percent, which is where it has been almost all of the time since the question was first asked by Gallup in 1987 (Gallup n.d.).

There was very little negative media coverage of Canada's failure to support its southern neighbor. "Canada's refusal to join war in Iraq draws US criticism" (Cohen 2003) was the headline of an Associated Press story that ran the day when US Ambassador to Canada, Paul Cellucci, stated, "There is a lot of disappointment in Washington and a lot of people are upset." Reports of Canadian hockey fans booing the American national anthem at games played in Montreal and Vancouver in the days following the invasion of Iraq received some mentions in the American media (Caldwell 2003), as did President Bush's 2004 visit to Canada. "Forecast Frosty for U.S.-Canadian Ties" (Struck 2004) and "Demonstrators greet Bush in Canada" (Bumiller 2004) were typical headlines in the elite American press. It is highly doubtful that any of this very limited coverage percolated down to influence American public opinion. Moreover, there is no evidence of American government retaliation against Canada for either the decision not to support the United States in Iraq or, two years later, the Canadian government's refusal to participate in a satellite-based system of continental anti-missile defense. In the longer term, however, such decisions may have contributed, among Washington policy-makers, to an image of Canada as a sometimes wobbly ally.

National Images Matter . . . Within Limits

The influence of American images of Canada on that country's politics and policy, and of Canadian images of the United States on Canada's politics and policy, might be summed up as follows. *The images held by Americans about Canada have seldom been a factor, and even less often a decisive factor, shaping American policy, whereas Canadians' images of the United States and of Americans often have had an important, and sometimes even a crucial influence on policies both domestic and foreign.* This is, however, too simplistic. It fails to acknowledge differences between the images held by elites and those held by the general population in each country, as well as the important variation across issues in the impact of national images.

In the case of Canadian cultural nationalism, this was driven by cultural and state elites who viewed American mass culture as a threat to Canadian identity and, ultimately, to the country's independence. Their enthusiasm for policies intended to promote what they have believed to be distinctively Canadian values and stories has never been embraced by the general public, as the media consumption preferences of Canadians have made clear. While there is no reason to doubt that the nationalist elites who have clamored for protectionism and subsidies of various sorts have genuinely believed that the American media have posed a sort of existential threat to their country, it is also the case that Canadian cultural producers have stood to gain economically from the myriad forms of state support that they have received for more than half a century. Sorting out material motivations from other factors, including images of the United States as a threat to Canadian culture and identity, will always be a matter of disagreement.

American state officials whose positions involve US–Canada relations have been aware of Canadian cultural nationalism since the days of the Massey Commission and its recommendations for much greater state support of and involvement in the cultural life of the nation. But with the notable exception of the split-edition issue and the taxation treatment of American-based magazines selling in the Canadian market, such policies as Canadian content requirements for broadcasters and subsidies for the Canadian film and television industries have not been sources of concern from the American side. The split-run issue became an important conflict between the Canadian and American governments in the late 1990s, when American officials, representing the interests of their country's magazine publishers, saw this as a strictly economic and trade issue. If there was an image of Canada that was part of American opposition to what was seen as discriminatory treatment of American cultural producers, it was of a country that was not willing to play by the rules of international trade and in which Canadian nationalist elites, "believed that the United States had an overarching agenda to systematically break down Canada's cultural protections" (Stewart, ibid., p. 44). There is no evidence that the American public was aware of this conflict, nor of Canadian cultural nationalism more generally.

More recently, the Canadian government's passage in 2023 of *The Online News Act*, requiring such social media giants as Meta and Google to pay Canadian news publishers for the use of their content, generated quite a lot of opposition from these American-based companies. It received very little coverage in the American media and, unlike the case of the earlier split-run issue, there has appeared to be little in the way of political push-back from American politicians and the US government. Support for the Canadian law from Democratic Senator Amy Klobuchar (Minnesota) and a rather tepid statement from the American Embassy in Ottawa that US officials are "continuing to watch developments" regarding the law's implementation and that Canadian officials should "consider U.S. stakeholder input" (Ty Roush 2023) were a far cry from the concern that Washington expressed over the split-run issue many years earlier.

As was true of cultural nationalism, the ascendence of economic nationalism in Canada during the mid-1950s began as an almost exclusively elite concern that was based on an image of the United States as a threat to Canadian independence, but also to the country's prosperity. In the past, such concerns had focused mainly on trade with the United States and recurrent fears that a free trade agreement would undermine Canadian sovereignty. The economic nationalism that was so central to the Canadian political conversation during the 1960s and 1970s, however, was focused on the issue of American direct ownership in the Canadian economy.

Although the Canadian public initially did not seem particularly moved by these new economic nationalist arguments, within a decade polls found that the image of American investment as a threat to Canada was held by a majority of Canadians. In view of the fact that, to varying degrees, all three major national political parties supported limits on foreign ownership – close to 80 percent of which was American – and that the issue was given prominence by reports of government commissions and task forces, as well as the media, it is not surprising that public opinion followed where elite opinion led. Nationalist policies intended to limit foreign ownership, ensure that it delivered benefits for Canadians, and increase Canadian ownership in certain sectors of the economy, particularly energy, found a receptive audience with much of the general public.

The more assertive economic nationalism in Canada was immediately noticed by state elites in Washington, as well as by industry leaders and prominent American economists. While sensitive to the need of Canadian governments to respond to the rising tide of concern over the level of American ownership in Canada, this concern and the policies that it spawned contributed to an American image of Canada as a country whose insecure identity relationship with the United States, rather than legitimate economic fears, were driving politics and policy. They pushed back against such policies as the Foreign Investment Review Act[14] and the National Energy Program, both of which were essentially dismantled by the mid-1980s. This image was held by some American state and economic elites, not by the general public. Most Americans were unaware that a majority of Canadians had come to view their corporations and the investment dollars they brought to Canada as a threat to Canadian independence.

Images of the United States were at the heart of the Canadian conversation – family feud might be a more apt characterization – over the proposal for a free trade agreement between the United States and Canada. From 1984, when the Macdonald Commission recommended that Canada seek such an agreement with its major trading partner, through the 1988 federal election, and even for several years after the pro-free trade Conservative Party was re-elected and proceeded to implement the treaty, opponents of free trade portrayed the United States as an existential threat to Canadian jobs, social programs, culture, and political sovereignty. The image of America held by those in Canada who supported the free trade agreement was much more benign, not ascribing to the United States the threatening qualities that were so central to the anti-free trade coalition. This was an issue, and 1988 was an election, where Canadian images of the United States, held by elites and the general public alike, had significant consequences.

The *sturm und drang* in Canada over free trade was not matched in the United States. The issue received very little coverage in the media, the major exceptions being occasional articles in the elite national press, particularly reports in the *New York Times* and *Washington Post* that acknowledged the fight that was taking place during Canada's 1988 election. State and some industry elites followed the course of the debate in Canada, but their views had much to do with economic considerations and little to do with what could be described as an image of Canada. This may be seen in two Brookings publications from 1987, based on conferences that brought together politicians, economists, and industry specialists from both sides of the border. Both books focused on legal and economic aspects of the agreement, and both were supportive of free trade (Stern et al. 1987; Macdonald and Fried 1987). No national survey of Americans' opinion on the proposed agreement was undertaken in the years leading up to its implementation in 1989, suggesting that the American public was by and large unaware of what in Canada was considered to be a crucial transition point in the country's history.[15]

The Canadian government's decision not to support the American-led invasion of Iraq was also strongly influenced by images of the United States held by much of the Canadian population, and by some elites. There was a widely held view that the United States was something of a bully on the international stage, with unilateralist instincts, and motives other than those given by the Bush administration. It is almost certainly true that these views of America were magnified by Canadians' widespread dislike of the Bush administration. But it is also the case that Canadians were used to thinking of their country and its approach to geo-politics as being premised on different values from those which they believed prevailed in the United States. Peacekeeping, multilateralism, soft power, and even anti-militarism – strongest in Quebec – were believed by Canadians to be the hallmarks of their country's approach to the world and to the resolution of its international conflicts. Canadian political leaders had for years told the public that these were ways in which their country differed from its southern neighbor.

At the same time, Canadian opinion on the war and the justifications offered for it was divided. It is entirely conceivable that had the Conservative Party formed the government, without a large number of MPs elected from Quebec, the Canadian government might have reached a different decision. The nature of Canada's electoral and party systems magnified the influence of Quebeckers' views on this issue. The fact that Prime Minister Jean Chrétien was dubious about American motives on the world stage, and certainly in the Middle East, also weighed against Canadian support for the United States.

Although the US Ambassador in Ottawa, Paul Cellucci, expressed public disappointment and even a sense of betrayal by a family member – and in this he doubtless echoed views in the White House and the State Department – it is almost certainly the case that relatively few Americans knew about Canada's decision. It is possible, however, that the Canadian government's refusal to support the invasion may have reinforced the view among state elites in Washington that Canadian support for American geo-political positions could not automatically be assumed and, moreover, that Canada might not always be a reliable partner on security issues. Combined with other security disagreements, including Canada's long-standing refusal to take seriously Washington's complaint that it spent too little on defense, and the Liberal government's 2005 decision not to participate in the space-based continental missile defense system being developed by the United States (Rudd 2005), it may be that the decision on Iraq was just one more dot on a line that eventually led to the 2021 announcement of AUKUS, the trilateral security pact between Australia, the United Kingdom, and the United States that, to the dismay of many Canadian commentators, excludes Canada (Berthiaume 2023).

National images matter. They certainly have had an influence on relations between the United States and Canada, particularly on the Canadian side. The extent of that influence will always be a matter of conjecture. Moreover, it is usually the case that other factors, including economic and security interests, and each country's domestic political culture, will weigh more heavily in the balance as determinants of its relationship with another country than whatever information, ideas, and sentiments comprise its image of the other. The sheer density of ties in trade, investment, communications, people, institutions, and state-to-state agreements that link the United States and Canada, to say nothing of geography, ensure that President Kennedy's famous 1961 declaration that "[w]hat unites us is far greater than what divides us," remains true. But as the political disagreements and policy conflicts discussed in this chapter show, there is still ample room for images of the other to influence outcomes.

Notes

1 Student militants loyal to the revolutionary Islamic government stormed the embassy, but the record is clear that the Iranian militia tasked with guarding the embassy put up no resistance and that within days, the Ayatollah Khomeini was publicly endorsing the action and the hostage-taking. Beyond these facts, it is unclear whether the government had given a green light to the militants.
2 In fact, the country's experience in World War I when, despite having a population of under ten million, more than 600,000 Canadians served in the military, over 400,000 troops were sent overseas, and about 61,000 Canadians were killed, marked the beginnings of a sense of Canadian nationalism that was not dependent on the British connection.
3 The United Kingdom exceeded Canada between 1940 and 1944 because British purchases from the United States were financed by the Lend-Lease policy.
4 This "golden era" of the Canada–US special relationship is described by some of Canada's foremost diplomats, including Allan Gotlieb (1981–89) and Charles Ritchie (1962–66) in their respective memoirs of their time as Canadian ambassadors in Washington, and Lester Pearson, who was Canada's Secretary of State for External Affairs (1948–57) before becoming leader of the Liberal Party of Canada.
5 There are dissenters from this view of greater Canadian deference. See, for example, Nevitte and Kanji (2003).
6 This well-known aphorism is attributed to John Aird, the chairman of the Royal Commission on Broadcasting, whose 1929 report recommended a major role for the state in Canada's fledgling broadcasting system.
7 In response to the dramatic rise in Canadian housing prices in 2021–22, the Canadian government passed a law imposing a two-year ban on non-Canadian persons and companies purchasing residential properties. Most of the coverage of what was widely believed to be foreign investors' role in driving up home prices focused on China, not on the United States. Fairly or not, has been clear for many years now that China has replaced the United States when fears about the impact of foreign investment arise.
8 Quebecers and French-language elites in that province were more likely than their counterparts in the rest of the country to support free trade with the United States.
9 Although the Liberal government that established the Macdonald Commission did not do so in the expectation that its major recommendation would be a free trade agreement with the United States, the scale of the Commission, producing 72 research studies and enlisting the services of many of the country's major economists, and the enormous controversy that followed, had no parallel in the United States. Whereas free trade was framed as an existential issue in Canada, as had always been the case when closer integration with the United States was proposed, it was barely on the radar screen south of the border.
10 Many of these political cartoons are archived at the McCord Stewart Museum and may be viewed online: www.musee-mccord-stewart.ca/en/.
11 "Hockey Night in Canada" has been for decades Canada's most-watched television program. Although statistical confirmation is hard to come by, it is widely believed that the program's viewership spiked during "Coach's Corner," shown between the first and second periods of each week's Saturday night hockey game. Cherry's popularity was such that he finished seventh in a 2004 poll asking who was the greatest Canadian of all time, edging out the country's first prime minister, John A. Macdonald. The video of Cherry's passionate on-air criticism of what he characterized as the Canadian government's

betrayal of its best friend and ally was removed from the CBC's online archive two weeks after it was recorded, the only episode of that program ever to be censored. http://static.espn.go.com/nhl/news/2003/0404/1533887.html.

12 Francophone Quebeckers were considerably less supportive of Canadian military involvement in Afghanistan beginning just months after the attacks of 9/11 until the end of Canada's mission in that country. See Kirton and Guebert (2007, 14–18).

13 Unfortunately, I have not been able to locate a record of this particular news story. It remains, however, vivid in my memory.

14 The Canadian government continues to have in place a process for reviewing certain foreign investments in Canada, under the Investment Canada Act. However, the scope of this review process and its aims have changed considerably from those that characterized the previous Foreign Investment Review Act. There is now a focus on what the Act refers to as "review of investments in Canada by non-Canadians that could be injurious to national security." Fear of American investment has been replaced, to a considerable degree, by concern over Chinese investments in natural resource and technology sectors of the Canadian economy.

15 I am unable to find any such survey.

REFERENCES

Allan, Chantal. 2009. *"Bomb Canada" and Other Unkind Remarks in the American Media.* Edmonton, Alberta: Athabasca University Press.

Allen, Cleo Joffrion. 2005. *Foreign News Coverage in Selected U.S. Newspapers 1927–1997: A Content Analysis.* Doctoral dissertation, Louisiana State University.

Allport, Gordon W. 1954. *The Nature of Prejudice.* New York: Doubleday.

Allsop, Jon. 2022. "The 'freedom convoy' and the press," *Columbia Journalism Review*, February 15: www.cjr.org/the_media_today/freedom_convoy_fox_media.php

Angus, H.F. and R.M. MacIver, eds. 1938. *Canada and Her Great Neighbour: Sociological Surveys of Opinions and Attitudes in Canada Concerning the United States.* Toronto: The Ryerson Press; New Haven: Yale University Press.

Angus Reid Institute. 2017. *Foreign Direct Investment in Canada: Who's Favoured, Who's Frowned Upon?* September 12: https://angusreid.org/foreign-direct-investment/

Angus Reid Institute. 2022. "Angst of the Americas: Four-in-five Canadians worry about the domestic impacts of continued U.S. Political Turmoil," *Angus Reid Institute*, February 9: https://angusreid.org/wp-content/uploads/2022/02/2022.02.09_US_Can_Democracy.pdf

Asia-Pacific Foundation of Canada. 2019. *2019 National Opinion Poll: Canadian Views on High-tech Investment from Asia*, June 12: www.asiapacific.ca/surveys/national-opinion-polls/2019-national-opinion-poll-canadian-views-high-tech

Assumption University. 2004. *Transcript of Martin Sheen's Speech on the Occasion of being Awarded the Christian Cultural Medal.* Assumption University, Windsor.

Atwood, Margaret. 1972. *Surfacing.* Toronto: McClelland & Stewart.

Atwood, M. (1986). Through the One-Way Mirror. In *The Nation (New York, N.Y.)* (Vol. 242, Issue 11, pp. 332–334). Nation Company L.P.

Aykroyd, Peter. 1992. *The Anniversary Compulsion: Canada's Centennial Celebrations, A Model Mega-Anniversary.* Toronto: Dundurn Press.

Azzi, Stephen. 1999. *Walter Gordon and the Rise of Canadian Nationalism.* Montreal: McGill-Queen's Press.

Baker, William M. 1973. "The Anti-American ingredient in Canadian history," *Dalhousie Review*, Vol. 53, No. 1, 57–77.

Bannister, Jennifer. 2017. *The American gaze: Adam Gopnik's Canada*, May 29: https://earlycanadianhistory.ca/2017/05/29/the-american-gaze-adam-gopniks-canada/

Banting, Keith, Jack Nagel, Chelsea Schafer and Daniel Westlake. 2019. "Assessing Performance: National Versus Regional Patterns," In Paul Quirk, ed., *Canada and the United States: How Two Democracies Differ and Why It Matters*. Toronto: Oxford University Press, 290–320.

BBC. 2015. *End 'Gross Indignity', Greek FM Varoufakis Tells Germany*, February 5: www.bbc.com/news/world-europe-31147112

Beam, Alex. 2006. "Nova Scotia, Mon Amour," *Atlantic Monthly*, January/February. https://www.theatlantic.com/magazine/archive/2006/01/nova-scotia-mon-amour/304519/

Beauvoir, Simone de. 1999. *America Day by Day* (Translated from *L'Amérique au jour le jour*, 1947, by Carol Cosman). Oakland, CA: University of California Press.

Bélanger, Damien-Claude. 2000. "French Canadian emigration to the United States 1840–1930," *Quebec History*: http://faculty.marianopolis.edu/c.belanger/quebechistory/readings/leaving.htm

Belch, Christopher M. 2004. *A View from Abroad: An Analysis of Canadian Coverage in U.S. Newspapers*. MA dissertation, University of Windsor.

Bender, P. 1883. "A Canadian view of annexation," *The North American Review*, Vol. 136, No. 317, 326–336.

Berger, Carl. 1972. "Comments on the carnegie series," In Richard A. Preston, ed., *The Influence of the United States on Canadian Development: Eleven Case Studies*. Durham, NC: Duke University Press.

Bergeron, François. 2017. "Un siècle de photos du New York Times au Canada," *L'Express*, September 13: https://l-express.ca/un-siecle-de-photos-du-new-york-times-au-canada/

Berkowitz, Irene. 2021. *Mediaucracy: Why Canada Hasn't Made Global TV Hits and How It Can*. Toronto: Ryerson University Pressbooks.

Berthiaume, Lee. 2023. "Canada on sidelines as U.S., Britain, Australia move ahead on new security deal," *Canadian Press*, March 13: www.cbc.ca/news/politics/aukus-national-defence-britain-australia-1.6777498

Berton, Pierre. 1975. *Hollywood's Canada: The Americanization of Our National Image*. Toronto: McClelland and Stewart.

Berton, Pierre. 1982. *Why We Act Like Canadians*. Toronto: McClelland and Stewart.

Bickerton, James. 2006. "Lament: The anguished conservatism of George Grant," In Bickerton James, Stephen Brooks and Alain-G. Gagnon, eds., *Freedom, Equality, Community: The Political Philosophy of Six Influential Canadians*. Montreal: McGill-Queen's University Press.

Blackadar, Kerry Jean. 2007. *A Content Analysis of US Newspaper Coverage of Canada and the UK's Healthcare Systems during America's Healthcare Reform*. Doctoral Dissertation submitted to the University of British Columbia.

Blatchford, Andy. 2022. "How Canada became America's New Culture War," *Politico*, February 27: www.politico.com/news/2022/02/27/canada-america-culture-war-protests-00012098

Blegen, Theodore C. 1918. "A plan for the Union of British North America and the United States, 1866," *The Mississippi Valley Historical Review*, Vol. 4, No. 4, 470–483.

Bliss, Michael. 1987. *Northern Enterprise: Five Centuries of Canadian Business*. Toronto: McClelland and Stewart.

Boulding, Kenneth E. 1959. "National images and international systems," *Journal of Conflict Resolution*, Vol. 3, No. 2, 120–131.

Boulet-Gercourt, Philippe. 2012. "L'Amérique qu'on aime et celle qui nous fait peur," *Le Nouvel Observateur*, October 17: www.nouvelobs.com/monde/presidentielle-us-2012/20121017.OBS5991/l-amerique-qu-on-aime-et-celle-qui-nous-fait-peur.html

Bourque, J.C. and Joe Martin. 2013. "How John F. Kennedy helped Diefenbaker lose an election," *Globe and Mail*, April 8. https://www.theglobeandmail.com/news/politics/how-john-f-kennedy-helped-diefenbaker-lose-an-election/article10844078/

Brebner, John Bartlet. 1937. *The Neutral Yankees of Nova Scotia*. New York: Columbia University Press.

Bretherton, Cyril. 1926. "Is Canada being Americanized?" *Maclean's*, March 15. https://archive.org/details/Macleans-Magazine-1926-03-15

Brock, Jared. 2018. "The story of Josiah Henson, the real inspiration for 'Uncle Tom's Cabin,'" *Smithsonian Magazine*, May 16: www.smithsonianmag.com/history/story-josiah-henson-real-inspiration-uncle-toms-cabin-180969094/

Broege, Valerie. 1986. "War with the United States in Canadian literature and visual arts," *Journal of American Culture*, Vol. 9, No. 1.

Brookes, Alan A. 1976. "Out-migration from the maritime provinces, 1860–1900: Some preliminary considerations," *Acadiensis*, Vol. 5, No. 2, 26–55.

Brooks, Stephen, ed. 2019. *Promoting Canadian Studies Abroad: Soft Power and Cultural Diplomacy*. London: Palgrave MacMillan.

Brooks, Stephen and Alain-G. Gagnon. 1988. *Social Scientists and Politics in Canada: Between Clerisy and Vanguard*. Montreal: McGill-Queen's University Press.

Brunet-Jailly, Emmanuel. 2006. "North American linkages: Leader survey on Canada-US Cross-Border regions: An analysis, " *Policy Research Initiative*. https://www.researchgate.net/publication/301649329_North_American_Linkages_Leader_Survey_on_Canada-US_Cross-Border_Regions_An_Analysis

Buchanan, William and Hadley Cantril. 1953. *How Nations See Each Other: A Study in Public Opinion*. Urbana, IL: University of Illinois Press.

Buckner, Phillip. 2020. "The Canadian Civil Wars of 1837–1838," *London Journal of Canadian Studies*, Vol. 35, No. 1, 96–118: https://doi.org/10.14324/111.444.ljcs.2020v35.005

Bukowczyk, John J., Nora Faires, David R. Smith and Randy William Widdis. 2005. *Permeable Border: The Great Lakes Basin as Transnational Region, 1650–1990*. Pittsburgh, PA: University of Pittsburgh Press.

Bumiller, Elisabeth. 2004. "Demonstrators greet Bush in Canada," *New York Times*, November 30: www.nytimes.com/2004/11/30/politics/demonstrators-greet-bush-in-canada.html

Bumsted, J.M. 1986. "Canada and American culture in the 1950s," In J.M. Bumsted, ed., *Interpreting Canada's Past*. Toronto: Oxford University Press.

Burkholder, Richard. 2003. "Unwilling coalition? Majorities in Britain, Canada oppose military action in Iraq," *Gallup*, February 18: https://news.gallup.com/poll/7798/unwilling-coalition-majorities-britain-canada-oppose-military-act.aspx

Cairns, Alan. 1992. "The charter: A political science perspective," *Osgoode Hall Law Journal*, Vol. 30, No. 3, 615–625.

Caldwell, David. 2003. "Canadiens issue apology for fans booing anthem," *New York Times*: www.nytimes.com/2003/03/22/sports/hockey-canadiens-issue-apology-for-fans-booing-anthem.html

Callaghan, Morley. 1958. "Go easy," *Maclean's*, June 7: https://archive.macleans.ca/article/1958/06/07/go-easy

Canadian Press. 2015. "JFK secretly sent electoral agents into Canada to help elect the Liberals," *National Post*, January 25: https://nationalpost.com/news/politics/what-did-john-f-kennedy-do-for-the-history-of-canada-plenty-experts-say

Caves, Richard. 1960. "United States-Canadian economic relations: The search for a home-owned soul," *Journal of International Affairs*, Vol. 14, No. 2, 175–186.
CBC News. 2016. *What Canadians Think of Americans*, March 10: www.youtube.com/watch?v=P-u3o2hvdUg
CBC News. 2019. *Imagining Canada*: https://l-express.ca/un-siecle-de-photos-du-new-york-times-au-canada/
Cellucci, Ambassador Paul. 2003. *Speech given to the Economic Club of Toronto*, March 25. https://policyoptions.irpp.org/wp-content/uploads/sites/2/assets/po/canada-and-the-iraq-war/cellucci.pdf
Chamberlain, Joseph Edgar. 1884. "The foreign elements in our population," *The Century; A Popular Quarterly*, Vol. 28, No. 5, 761–771.
Chrétien, Jean. 2018. *My Stories, My Times*. Toronto: Random House.
Coates, Colin. 2015. "If Stephen Harper doesn't support Canadian Studies, why should we?" *Active History*, June 4. https://activehistory.ca/blog/2015/06/04/if-stephen-harper-doesnt-support-canadian-studies-why-should-we/
Cohen, Andrew. 1983. "Robinson says the U.S. Did not demand Canada change policies," *United Press International*, March 13: www.upi.com/Archives/1983/03/13/Robinson-says-the-US-did-not-demand-Canada-change-policies/3096416379600/
Cohen, Tom. 2003. "Canada's refusal to join war in Iraq draws U.S. Criticism," *Associated Press*, March 26: www.semissourian.com/story/104991.html
Cohen, Warren. 1973. "American perceptions of China," In Michel Oksenberg and Robert B. Oxnam, eds., *Dragon and Eagle: United States-China Relations, Past and Future*. New York: Basic Books.
Colleto, David. 2022. "David Coletto free trade at 35: Canadian public opinion, then and now," *Canadian Politics and Public Policy*, September-October, 32–33: www.policymagazine.ca/wp-content/uploads/2022/09/Policy_Mag-Sept-Oct_Lr.pdf
Continental Congress. 1774. *Address to the People of Great Britain*, October 21. https://founders.archives.gov/documents/Jay/01-01-02-0071
Coren, Michael. 2022. "'Freedom Convoy' shows the Americanisation of Canada's right," *The New Statesman*, January 28: www.newstatesman.com/international-politics/democracy-international-politics/2022/01/freedom-convoy-shows-the-americanisation-of-canadas-right
Craven, Margaret H. 1938. *Canadian-American Commerce: A Study of Trade Relations between Canada and the United States from 1846 to the Present*. Thesis for the B.A. Degree, Honours in Political Economy, McMaster University.
Creighton, Donald. 1937. *The Commercial Empire of the St. Lawrence, 1760–1850*. Toronto: Ryerson Press.
Cuddy, A.J., Fiske S.T. and Glick P. 2007. "The BIAS map: Behaviors from intergroup affect and stereotypes," *Journal of Personality and Social Psychology*, Vol. 92, No. 4, 631–648.
Curti, M. and Birr K. 1950. "The immigrant and the American image in Europe, 1860–1914," *The Mississippi Valley Historical Review*, Vol. 37, No. 2, 203–230: https://doi.org/10.2307/1892129
Dafoe, John Wesley. 1935. *Canada, an American Nation*. New York: Columbia University Press.
Dagenais, Maxime. 2017. "Hunters' lodges," *The Canadian Encyclopedia*: www.thecanadianencyclopedia.ca/en/article/hunters-lodges
Danisch, Robert. 2022. "Canada should be preparing for the end of American democracy," *The Conversation*, February 13: https://theconversation.com/canada-should-be-preparing-for-the-end-of-american-democracy-176930

Datta, Monti. 2020. "What Iranians think of the US and their own government," *The Conversation*, January 15: https://theconversation.com/what-iranians-think-of-the-us-and-their-own-government-129400

Davies, Helen. 1999. *The Politics of Participation: A Study of Canada's Centennial Celebration*. Ph.D. dissertation, University of Manitoba.

De Beauvoir, Simone. 1999. *America Day by Day* (Originally published in 1947 as *L'Amérique au jour le jour*. Translated by Carole Cosman). Oakland, CA: University of California Press.

Dobson, Wendy. 2002. *Shaping the Future of the North American Economic Space*. Toronto: C.D. Howe Institute.

Doran, Charles F. and James Patrick Sewell. 1988. "Anti-Americanism in Canada?" *The Annals of the American Academy of Political and Social Science*, Vol. 497, 105–19.

Dovidio, J.F., Hewstone M., Glick P. and Esses V.M. 2010. "Prejudice, stereotyping and discrimination: Theoretical and empirical overview," In J.F. Dovidio, M. Hewstone, P. Glick and V.M. Esses, eds., *The SAGE Handbook of Prejudice, Stereotyping and Discrimination*, 3–29. London: Sage Publications.

Drew, Benjamin. 1856. *A North-Side View of Slavery. The Refugee: Or the Narratives of Fugitive Slaves in Canada. Related by Themselves, with an Account of the History and Condition of the Colored Population of Upper Canada*. Boston: John P. Jewett and Company.

Duhamel, Georges. 1931. *America the Menace: Scenes from Life of the Future* (Translated by Charles Miner Thompson). Boston: Houghton Mifflin.

Earle, Renee M. 2020. "International opinion of the U.S. Slides from respect to pity," *American Diplomacy*, August: https://americandiplomacy.web.unc.edu/2020/08/international-opinion-of-the-u-s-slides-from-respect-to-pity/

Edmonston, Barry. 2016. "Canada's immigration trends and patterns," *Canadian Studies in Population*, Vol. 43, No. 1–2, 78–116.

Edwardson, Ryan. 2008. *Canadian Content: Culture and the Quest for Nationhood*. Toronto: University of Toronto Press.

Enders, Adam, Steven Smallpage and Robert Lupton. 2020. "Are all 'birthers' conspiracy theorists? On the relationship between conspiratorial thinking and political orientations," *British Journal of Political Science*, Vol. 50, No. 3, 849–866.

Environics. 1986/1989. "A poll taken in September of that year, cited in Lawrence Leduc and J. Alex Murray, "Open for Business? Foreign Investment and Trade Issues in Canada," footnote 5 at page 138," In Gary Zuk, Harold Clarke and Marianne Stewart, eds., *Economic Decline and Political Change: Canada, Great Britain and the United States*. Pittsburgh: University of Pittsburgh Press.

Environics. 2022. *The Evolution of the Canadian Identity*: www.environicsinstitute.org/projects/project-details/the-evolution-of-the-canadian-identity

Ericsson, Samuel. 1954. *Are Canadians Really?* Washington, DC: Chamber of Commerce of the United States.

Fairlie, Henry. 1988. "What Europeans Thought of Our Revolution," *The New Republic*, July 18: https://newrepublic.com/article/118527/american-revolution-what-did-europeans-think

Fält, Olavi K. 1995. "The historical study of mental images," *Comparative Civilizations Review*, Vol. 32, No. 32, Article 6.

Fellows, Jo-Ann. 1971. "The Loyalist Myth in Canada," *Historical Papers/Communications Historiques*, Vol. 6, No. 1, 94–111: https://doi.org/10.7202/030459ar

Ferris-Rotman, Amie. 2011. "Nazi jokes, wrath at Germans highlight Greek despair," *Reuters*, October 26: www.reuters.com/article/greece-germany-relations-idUSL5E7LQ2LL20111026

Foster, Kate. 1926. *Our Canadian Mosaic*. Toronto: YWCA Dominion Council.

Foyle, D.C. 1997. "Public opinion and foreign policy: Elite beliefs as a mediating variable," *International Studies Quarterly*, Vol. 41, No. 1, 141–169: www.jstor.org/stable/2600910

Francis, Diane. 2013. *Merger of the Century: Why Canada and America Should become One Country*. Toronto: HarperCollins.

Fried, Edward R., Frank Stone and Philip H. Trezise, eds. 1987. *Building a Canadian-American Free Trade Area*. Washington, DC: Brookings Institution.

Frum, David. 2018. *Trumpocracy: The Corruption of the American Republic*. New York: Harper.

Fulford, Robert. 1970. "The new Anti-Americanism," *Saturday Night*, March [Reprinted in Hugh Innis, ed., *Americanization*. Toronto: McGraw-Hill, Ryerson], 18–20.

Gallup. n.d. *Country Ratings*: https://news.gallup.com/poll/1624/perceptions-foreign-countries.aspx

Gambino, Megan. 2011. "The unknown contributions of Brits in the American Civil War: Historian Amanda Foreman discusses how British citizens took part in the war between the Union and the Confederacy," *The Smithsonian Magazine*, December 9. https://www.smithsonianmag.com/history/the-unknown-contributions-of-brits-in-the-american-civil-war-2478471/

Gasher, Mike. 1998. "Invoking public support for public broadcasting: The Aird commission revisited," *Canadian Journal of Communication*, Vol. 23, No. 2.

Gibbon, John Murray. 1938. *Canadian Mosaic: The Making of a Northern Nation*. Toronto: McClelland and Stewart.

Gilmore, Scott. 2017. "The American dream has moved to Canada," *Maclean's*, February 28: www.theglobeandmail.com/opinion/article-searching-for-the-american-dream-go-to-canada/

Globe and Mail. 1986. "That American Model," *Globe and Mail*, unsigned editorial, February 7. Quoted in Doran and Sewell (1988), 118.

Globerman, Steven. 2008. *The Impacts of 9/11 on Canada-U.S. Trade*. Toronto: University of Toronto Press.

Gopnik, Adam. 2017. "We could have been Canada," *The New Yorker*, May 15: www.newyorker.com/magazine/2017/05/15/we-could-have-been-canada

Gotlieb, Alan. 1987. *Some Canadian Myths about the United States*. Toronto: Empire Club.

Gotlieb, Alan. 2002. "Why not a Grand Bargain with the U.S.?" *The National Post*, September 11, A16.

Government of Canada. 1951. *Final Report of the Royal Commission on National Development in the Arts, Letters and Sciences* (Generally referred to as the Massey Commission and the Massey Report). Ottawa: Government of Canada.

Government of Canada. 1957. *Final Report of the Royal Commission on Broadcasting*. Ottawa: Government of Canada.

Government of Canada. 1955. *Final Report of the Royal Commission on Canada's Economic Prospects*. Ottawa: Government of Canada.

Government of Canada. 1960. *Final Report of the Royal Commission on Publications*. Ottawa: Government of Canada.

Government of Canada. 1972. *Final Report of the Task Force on Foreign Ownership*. Ottawa: Government of Canada.

Granatstein, J.L. 1996. *Yankee Go Home? Canadians and Anti-Americanism*. Toronto: HarperCollins.

Granatstein, J.L. and Robert Bothwell. 1991. *Pirouette: Pierre Trudeau and Canadian Foreign Policy*. Toronto: University of Toronto Press.

Grant, George. 1970. *Lament for a Nation: The Defeat of Canadian Nationalism* (First published in 1965). Toronto: McClelland & Stewart.

Gravelle, Timothy. 2014. "Love thy neighbo(u)r? Political attitudes, proximity and the mutual perceptions of the Canadian and American publics," *Canadian Journal of Political Science*, Vol. 47, No. 1, 135–157: https://doi.org/10.1017/S0008423914000171

Green, Alan G., Mary MacKinnon and Chris Minns. 2002. "Dominion or Republic? Migrants to North America from the United Kingdom,1870–1910," *Economic History Review*, LV, Vol. 4, 666–696.

Gregg, Allan R. 2002. "Strains across the border," *Maclean's*, December 30, 32–36.

Haglund, David and Justin Massie. 2016. "Southern (over) exposure? Quebec and the evolution of Canada's grand strategy, 2002–2012," *American Review of Canadian Studies*, Vol. 46, No. 2, 233–253.

Haidt, Jonathan. 2012. *The Righteous Mind: Why Good People Are Divided by Politics and Religion*. New York: Pantheon Books.

Harrison, Trevor W. 2007. "Anti-Canadianism: Explaining the deep roots of a shallow phenomenon," *International Journal of Canadian Studies*, Vol. 35, 217–239.

Harper's (author not indicated). 1883. "The Canadian Habitant," *Harper's New Monthly Magazine*, Vol. 67, No. 399, 375–392.

Hart, E.J. 1983. *The Selling of Canada: The CPR and the Beginnings of Canadian Tourism*. Banff, Canada: Altitude Publishing Ltd.

Haynes, Frederick E. 1892. "The reciprocity treaty with Canada of 1854," *Published by the American Economic Association*, Vol. 7, No. 6, 7–70.

Hayward, Victoria. 1922. *Romantic Canada*. Toronto: Macmillan Company of Canada.

Hemingway, Ernest. 1926. I like Canadians: https://allpoetry.com/I-Like-Canadians

Hémon, Louis. 1921. *Maria Chapdelaine: A Tale of the Lake St. John Country* (First published in French in 1913 as *Maria Chapdelaine: Récit du Canada français*. Translated by W.H. Blake). New York: MacMillan: www.gutenberg.org/files/4383/4383-h/4383-h.htm

Henshaw, Peter. 2007. "John Buchan and the British imperial origins of Canadian multiculturalism," In Norman Hillmer and Adam Chapnick, eds., *Canadas of the Mind: The Making and Unmaking of Canadian Nationalisms in the Twentieth Century*. Montreal and Kingston: McGill-Queen's University Press, 191–213.

Hepburn, Sharon A. 1999. "Following the North Star: Canada as a Haven for Nineteenth-Century American Blacks," *Michigan Historical Review*, Vol. 25, No. 2, 91–126.

Hersko, Tyler. 2021. "'The Handmaid's Tale' Shoots to the Top of Nielsen's streaming ratings," *IndieWire*, June 18: www.indiewire.com/features/general/handmaids-tale-nielsen-streaming-ratings-1234645256/

Hollander, Paul. 1995. *Anti-Americanism: Irrational and Rational*. New York: Routledge.

Holsti, Ole R. 2004. *Public Opinion and American Foreign Policy*. Revised ed. Ann Arbor: University of Michigan Press.

Homer-Dixon, Thomas. 2022. "The American polity and might collapse: Canada must be prepared," *Globe and Mail*, January 1: www.theglobeandmail.com/opinion/article-the-american-polity-is-cracked-and-might-collapse-canada-must-prepare/

Horsman, Reginald. 1987. "On to Canada: Manifest destiny and United States strategy in the War of 1812," *Michigan Historical Review*, Vol. 13, No. 2, 1–24.

Howse, Allysha. 2019. "It's official, Canadians now make more money than Americans," *Narcity*, August 30: www.narcity.com/canadians-now-make-more-money-than-americans-new-study-shows

Hunt, Stephen. 2019. "U.S. Foundations funding Canadian anti-pipeline protests: Fair or foul?" *CBC News*, January 22: www.cbc.ca/news/canada/calgary/anti-pipeline-american-funding-protest-conspiracy-theory-1.4987202

Hutchison, Bruce. 1942. *The Unknown Country: Canada and her People*. New York: Coward-McCann.
Hutchison, Bruce. 1959. "Will the whole continent go Hollywood?" *Maclean's*, June 6: https://archive.macleans.ca/article/1959/6/6/will-the-whole-continent-go-hollywood
Igartua, José. 2006. *The Other Quiet Revolution: Nationalities in English Canada, 1945–1971*. Vancouver: University of British Columbia Press.
Innis, Harold. 1940. *The Cod Fisheries: The History of an International Economy*. New Haven, CT: Yale University Press.
Ipsos. 2002. *A Majority (56%) Believe Saddam Hussein Represents Real Threat to World Peace*: www.ipsos.com/en-ca/majority-56-believe-saddam-hussein-represents-real-threat-world-peace
Irwin, Douglas. 2019. "US trade policy in historical perspective," *National Bureau of Economic Research*: www.nber.org/papers/w26256
Isaacs, Harold. 1970. "Sources of images of foreign countries," In *Public Opinion and Historians*. Detroit: Wayne State University Press, 91–105.
Isaacs, Harold. 1972. *Images of Asia: American Views of China and India*. New York: Harper Torchbooks.
Isen, Tajja. 2022. "Why success in Canada means moving to America," *The Walrus*, May 30: https://thewalrus.ca/why-success-in-canada-means-moving-to-america/
Isernia, Pierangelo. 2007. "Anti-Americanism in Europe during the Cold War," In Robert O. Keohane and Peter J. Katzenstein, eds., *Anti-Americanisms in World Politics*. Ithaca, NY: Cornell University Press, 57–92.
Jackson, G.E. 1923. "Emigration of Canadians to the United States," *The Annals of the American Academy of Political and Social Science*, Vol. 107, 25–34: www.jstor.org/stable/1014691
Janigan, Mary, et al. 1988. "The numbers game," *Maclean's*, November 28: https://archive.macleans.ca/article/1988/11/28/the-numbers-game
Jones, David T. 2004. "When security Trumps economics: The new template of Canada-U.S. Relations," *Policy Options*, June-July: http://irpp.org/wp-content/uploads/assets/po/north-american-integration/jones.pdf
Kaufman, Michael. 1983. "Canada: An American discovers its difference," *The New York Times Magazine*, May 15. Reproduced in *Annual Editions: Comparative Politics 84/85* Dushkin Publishing Group, Inc., Sluice Dock Guilford, Ct., 1984, 165–167.
Kelly, Brendan. 2017. "The politician and the civil servant: Pierre Trudeau, Marcel Cadieux, and the Department of External Affairs, 1968–1970," *International Journal*, Vol. 72, No. 1,5–27: https://doi.org/10.1177/0020702017694212
Kennan, George. 1945. *The Long Telegram*: https://nsarchive2.gwu.edu/coldwar/documents/episode-1/kennan.htm
Kennedy, John F. 1961. *Address before the Canadian Parliament in Ottawa*, May 17: www.presidency.ucsb.edu/documents/address-before-the-canadian-parliament-ottawa
Keohane, Robert and Joseph Nye. 2012. *Power and Interdependence*. 4th ed. New York: Longman.
Khanna, Parag. 2021. "Searching for the American Dream? Go to Canada," *The Globe and Mail*, October 15: www.theglobeandmail.com/opinion/article-searching-for-the-american-dream-go-to-canada/
Kingwell, Mark. 2003. "What Distinguishes Us from Americans," *National Post*, March 5, A16.

Kirton, John and Jennilee Guebert. 2007. "Two solitudes, one war: Public opinion, national unity and Canada's war in Afghanistan," *Paper prepared for a Conference on "Quebec and War"*, Université de Québec à Montréal, Montreal, October 5–6.

Kirtz, Mary and Carol Beran. 2006. "My heart will go on living *la vida loca*," In *The Elections of 2000: Politics, Culture, and Economics in North America*. Akron, OH: University of Akron Press.

Kristoff, William. 2017. "Canada, leading the free world," *New York Times*, February 4: www.nytimes.com/2017/02/04/opinion/sunday/canada-leading-the-free-world.html

Kuznets, Simon. 1959. "Canada's Economic Prospects," *The American Economic Review*, Vol. 49, No. 3, 359–385.

Kymlicka, Will. 2007. *Multicultural Odysseys. Navigating the New International Politics of Diversity*. New York: Oxford University Press.

Lacroix, Patrick. 2017. "Finding Thoreau in French Canada: The ideological legacy of the American Revolution," *American Review of Canadian Studies*, Vol. 47, No. 3, 266–279: https://doi.org/10.1080/02722011.2017.1370719

Laski, Harold. 1948. *The American Democracy: A Commentary and an Interpretation*. New York: Viking Press.

Lauck, W. Jett. 1904. "The political significance of reciprocity," *Journal of Political Economy*, Vol. 12, No. 4, 495–524.

Laurier, Wilfrid. 1904. "Canada's century," *Great Canadian Speeches*: https://greatcanadianspeeches.ca/2020/06/29/wilfrid-laurier-canadas-century-1904/

Lebow, Richard Ned and Robert Kelly. 2001. "Thucydides and Hegemony: Athens and the United States," *Review of International Studies*, Vol. 27, No. 4, 593–609.

Leduc, Lawrence. 1989. "The Canadian Federal election of 1988," *Electoral Studies*, Vol. 8, No. 2, 163–167.

Leger Marketing. 2001. *A Study of How Canadians Perceive Canada-U.S. Relations*: www.legermarketing.com/documents/SPCLM/010910ENG.pdf

Lent, John. 1977. "Foreign News in American media," *Journal of Communication*, Vol. 27, No. 1, 46–51.

Levitz, Eric. 2022. "Why conservatives celebrate the Canadian truckers," *Intelligencer*, February 11: https://nymag.com/intelligencer/2022/02/conservatives-canadian-truckers-freedom-convoy.html

Library and Archives Canada. 2017. *The New El Dorado – Attracting Settlers to the West*, May 2: https://thediscoverblog.com/2017/05/02/the-new-el-dorado-attracting-settlers-to-the-west/

Ling, Justin. 2022. "Was it really about vaccine mandates – or something darker? The inside story of the convoy protests," *Toronto Star*, March 19. https://www.thestar.com/news/canada/was-it-really-about-vaccine-mandates-or-something-darker-the-inside-story-of-the-convoy/article_18a9dd13-2a65-59a3-b8d4-df3d8d9061c3.html

Lipset, Seymour Martin. 1990. *Continental Divide: The Values and Institutions of the United States and Canada*. New York: Routledge.

Little, Jack I. 2012. "'Like a fragment of the old world': The historical regression of Quebec City in travel narratives and Tourist Guidebooks, 1776–1913," *Urban History Review*, Vol. 40, No. 2, 15–27.

Lower, A.R.M. 1953. *Colony to Nation: A History of Canada*. Harlow: Longmans Green & Co.

Lower, A.R.M. 1958. "The gods Canadians worship," *Maclean's*, October 25: https://archive.macleans.ca/article/1958/10/25/the-gods-canadians-worship

Macdonald, D. S., & Fried, E. R. 1987. *Building a Canadian-American free trade area: Papers by Donald S. Macdonald . . . [et al.] presented at a conference at the Brookings Institution chaired by Bruce K. MacLaury on February 3, 1987*. Brookings Institution.

Mackay, Charles. 1876. *The Poetical Works of Charles Mackay: Now for the First Time Collected*, London: Frederick Warne & Co.

MacKay, R.A. 1937. "The political ideas of William Lyon Mackenzie," *The Canadian Journal of Economics and Political Science*, Vol. 3, No. 1, 1–22.

MacKenzie, David and Patrice Dutil. 2011. *Canada 1911: The Decisive Election that Shaped the Country*. Toronto: Dundurn Press.

MacKenzie, William Lyon. 1837. "The declaration of the reformers of the City of Toronto to their fellow reformers in Upper Canada," Toronto, August 2: https://web2.uvcs.uvic.ca/courses/lawdemo/DOCS/SNOW.HTM

MacLennan, Anne F. 2009. "American network broadcasting, the CBC, and Canadian radio stations during the 1930s: A content analysis," *Journal of Radio Studies*, Vol. 12, No. 1, 85–103.

MacLennan, Hugh. 1960. "It's the U.S. Or Us!" *Maclean's*, November 5: https://archive.macleans.ca/article/1960/11/05/its-the-us-or-us

Maltby, Richard. 2004. "Introduction," In Melvyn Stokes and Richard Maltby, eds., *Hollywood Abroad: Audiences and Cultural Exchange*. London: British Film Institute.

Manulak, Michael. 2011. *Canada and the Kosovo Crisis: An Agenda for Intervention*. Ontario, Canada: Centre for International Relations, Queen's University Kingston.

Markovits, Andrei. 2007. *Uncouth Nation: Why Europe Dislikes America*. Princeton, NJ: Princeton University Press.

Marsh, James. 2015. "Election 1891: A question of loyalty," In *The Canadian Encyclopedia*: www.thecanadianencyclopedia.ca/en/article/election-1891-a-question-of-loyalty-feature

Marshall, Peter. 1990. "George Bancroft on the Canadian rebellions and the American revolution." *The New England Quarterly*, Vol. 63, No. 2, 302–308.

Martin, Ged. 2004. *Past Futures: The Impossible Necessity of History*. Toronto: University of Toronto Press.

Martin, Paul. 2012. "Canada's image Abroad: Fade to black," *University Affairs*, June 12: www.universityaffairs.ca/opinion/in-my-opinion/canadas-image-abroad-fade-to-black/

Massie, Justin. 2008. "Regional strategic subcultures: Canadians and the use of force in Afghanistan and Iraq," *Canadian Foreign Policy Journal*, Vol. 14, No. 2, 19–48. https://www.tandfonline.com/doi/abs/10.1080/11926422.2008.9673461

Massie, Justin and David Haglund. 2012. "Le problème américain du Québec: differential de perceptions de la mendce dans la communauté de sécurité nord-américaine," Dans M. Riovx (dir), Débordement sécuritaire. Montréal: Éditors IEIM.

McRae, McRae. 1964. "The structure of Canadian history," In Louis Hartz, ed., *The Founding of New World Societies*. New York: Harcourt Brace & World.

McTague, Tom. 2020. "The decline of the American world," *The Atlantic*, June: www.theatlantic.com/international/archive/2020/06/america-image-power-trump/613228/

Mirrlees, Tanner. 2018. "Global Hollywood: An entertainment imperium, by integration," *Cineaction*, Vol. 99: https://cineaction.ca/issue-99/global-hollywood-an-entertainment-imperium-by-integration/

Miskell, Peter. 2014. "Hollywood films and foreign markets in the Studio Era: A fresh look at the evidence." *Discussion Paper, Henley Business School*, University of Reading.

Moens, Alexander and Nachum Gabler. 2011. "What congress thinks of Canada," In *Studies in Canada-U.S. Relations*. Vancouver: Fraser Institute.

Monière, Denis. 1981. *Ideologies in Quebec: The Historical Development*. Toronto: University of Toronto Press.

Moodie, Susanna. 2009. *Roughing it in the Bush* (First published in 1852). Toronto: Penguin.

Morrissey, Katherine. 1998. *Mental Territories: Mapping the Inland Empire*. Ithaca, NY: Cornell University Press.

Mortimer, Benjamin, Leslie R. Gray and John Heckewelder. 1954. "From Bethlehem to fairfield – 1798," *Transactions of the Moravian Historical Society*, Vol. 16, No. 1, 1–52.

Mowat, Farley. 1958. "Get tough," *Maclean's*, June 7: https://archive.macleans.ca/article/1958/06/07/get-tough

Murchison, Heather. 2008. *Unmasking Cultural Protectionism: An Analysis of the Relationship Between the Nation State and Culture in Contemporary Canada*. Ph.D thesis, London School of Economics and Political Science.

NATO. n.d. *Canada and NATO*: www.nato.int/cps/en/natohq/declassified_161511.htm\

NBC. 2010. *Tom Brokaw Explains Canada to Americans*, February 25: www.youtube.com/watch?v=lrA4V6YF6SA

Nelles, H.V. 2007. "Review of 'permeable border,'" *Michigan Historical Review*, Vol. 33, No. 1, 136–139.

Nevitte, Neil. 1996. *The Decline of Deference: Canadian Value Change in Cross-National Perspective*. Toronto: University of Toronto Press.

Nevitte, Neil and Mebs Kanji. 2003. "Who are the most deferential – Canadians or Americans?" In David M. Thomas, ed., *Canada and the United States: Differences that Count*. 4th ed. Toronto: University of Toronto Press, 121–140.

Newman, Peter C. 1956. "Who really owns Canada?" *Maclean's*, June 9: https://archive.macleans.ca/article/1956/6/9/who-really-owns-canada

Nielson, Carmen. 2016. "Erotic attachment, identity formation and the body politic: The woman-as-nation in Canadian graphic satire, 1867–1914," *Gender and History*, Vol. 28, No.1, 102–126.

Nixon, Richard. 1972. *Address to a Joint Meeting of the Canadian Parliament*, April 14: www.presidency.ucsb.edu/documents/address-joint-meeting-the-canadian-parliament

North American Review (author not identified). 1852. "Commercial Intercourse with British America," *North American Review*, Vol. 74.

Nye, Joseph S. *Soft Power: The Means to Success in World Politics*. 1st ed. New York: Public Affairs, 2004.

Obama, Barack. 2016. *Remarks by President Obama in Address to the Parliament of Canada*, June 29: https://obamawhitehouse.archives.gov/the-press-office/2016/06/30/remarks-president-obama-address-parliament-canada

Office of the Historian. 1953. *Memorandum for the President by the Secretary of State, No. 969*. May 6: https://history.state.gov/historicaldocuments/frus1952-54v06p2/d969

Office of the Historian. 1954. *The Chargé in Canada (Bliss) to the Department of State, No. 996*. August 19: https://history.state.gov/historicaldocuments/frus1952-54v06p2/d996

Office of the Historian. 1957a. *Despatch From the Embassy in Canada to the Department of State, No. 362*, March 1: https://history.state.gov/historicaldocuments/frus1955-57v27/d362

Office of the Historian. 1957b. *Telegram From the Embassy in Canada to the Department of State, No. 369*, June 11: https://history.state.gov/historicaldocuments/frus1955-57v27/d369

Office of the Historian. 1963a. *Telegram From the Embassy in Canada to the Department of State, No. 447*, April 15: https://history.state.gov/historicaldocuments/frus1961-63v13/d447

Office of the Historian. 1963b. *National Security Action Memorandum, No. 234*. April 18: https://history.state.gov/historicaldocuments/frus1961-63v13/d448

Office of the Historian. 1963c. *Telegram From the Department of State to the Embassy in Canada, No. 451*. June 28: https://history.state.gov/historicaldocuments/frus1961-63v13/d451

Oliver, Dean. n.d. "Canada and NATO," *Canadian War Museum*: www.warmuseum.ca/learn/dispatches/canada-and-nato/#tabs

Ouellet, Fernand. 1972. *Louis-Joseph Papineau: A Divided Soul*. Ottawa: Canadian Historical Association.

Paikin, Steve. 2022. "Is the U.S. on the verge of Civil War?" *The Agenda*, January 10: www.youtube.com/watch?v=cagQGM2abec

Paris, Roland. 2016. *The World Won't Wait: Why Canada Needs to Rethink its International Policies*. Toronto: University of Toronto Press.

Parker, D.W. 1911. "Secret reports of John Howe, 1808," *American Historical Review*, Vol. XVII, 332–354.

Parkman, Francis. 1892. *France and England in North America, Part IV: The Old Régime In Canada*. Boston: Little, Brown, and Company.

Paton, H.S. 1921. "Reciprocity with Canada. The Canadian Viewpoint," *The Quarterly Journal of Economics*, Vol. 35, No. 4, 574–595.

Peers, Frank. 1973. *The Politics of Canadian Broadcasting, 1920–1951*. Toronto: University of Toronto Press.

Peskin, Lawrence A. 2011. "Conspiratorial anglophobia and the war of 1812," *The Journal of American History*, Vol. 98, No. 3, 647–669: www.jstor.org/stable/41510113

Policy Options. 2003. "Pro-Canadian, Anti-American, or Anti-War? Canadian public opinion on the eve of the war," *Policy Options*, April 1: https://policyoptions.irpp.org/magazines/big-ideas/pro-canadian-anti-american-or-anti-war-canadian-public-opinion-on-the-eve-of-war/

Postmedia News. 2017. "Millions in foreign funds spent in 2015 federal election to defeat Harper Government, report alleges," *National Post*, May 23: https://nationalpost.com/news/politics/millions-in-foreign-funds-spent-in-2015-federal-election-to-defeat-harper-government-report-alleges

Potter, Evan. 2009. *Branding Canada: Projecting Canada's Soft Power through Public Diplomacy*. Montreal: McGill-Queen's University Press.

Ramirez, Bruno. 2001. "Canada in the United States: Perspectives on migration and continental history," *Journal of American Ethnic History*, Vol. 20, No. 3, 50–70.

Read, Colin. 1988. *The Rebellion of 1837 in Upper Canada*. Ottawa: Canadian Historical Association.

Remez, Michael and Richard Wike. 2008. "Global media celebrate Obama victory – But Cautious Too," *Pew Research Center*, November 13: www.pewresearch.org/global/2008/11/13/global-media-celebrate-obama-victory-but-cautious-too/

Revel, Jean-François. 2002. *L'obsession anti-américaine: Son fonctionnement, ses causes, ses inconséquences*. Paris: Éditions Plon.

Riddell, William Renwick. 1924. "Benjamin Franklin's mission to Canada and the causes of its failure," *The Pennsylvania Magazine of History and Biography*, Vol. 48, No. 2, 111–158.

Rioux, Jean-Sébastien. 2005. *Two Solitudes: Quebecers' Attitudes Regarding Canadian Security and Defence Policy*. Calgary: Canadian Defence and Foreign Affairs Institute.

Rodrick, Stephen. 2017. "Justin Trudeau: North Star," *Rolling Stone*, July 26: www.rollingstone.com/politics/politics-features/justin-trudeau-the-north-star-194313/

Rogan, Joe. 2022. *The Rogan Experience*, January 26, 2022: https://open.spotify.com/show/4rOoJ6Egrf8K2IrywzwOMk

Roger, Philippe. 2002. *L'Ennemi américain: Généologie de l'anti-américainisme français*. Paris: Editions du Seuil.

Rohdie, Sam. n.d. *Jean Paul Sartre, Hollywood, Citizen Kane, and La Nouvelle Vague*: www.screeningthepast.com/issue-38-first-release/jean-paul-sartre-hollywood-citizen-kane-and-the-french-nouvelle-vague/#:~:text=The%20love%20of%20the%20American,bias%2C%20its%20popularity%20and%20populism

Roush, Ty. 2023. "Canada-meta fight escalates: Canadian Government Halting Ads on Facebook and Instagram after meta removes news links," *Forbes*, July 5. https://www.forbes.com/sites/tylerroush/2023/07/05/canada-meta-fight-escalates-canadian-government-halting-ads-on-facebook-and-instagram-after-meta-removes-news-links/?sh=160136202759

Rudd, David. 2005. "Muddling through on missile defence: The politics of indecision," *Policy Options*, May: https://policyoptions.irpp.org/wp-content/uploads/sites/2/assets/po/defending-north-america/rudd.pdf

Rumer, Eugene and Richard Sokolsky. 2021. "Grand illusions: The impact of misperceptions about Russian on U.S. Policy," *Carnegie Endowment for International Peace*: https://carnegieendowment.org/2021/06/30/grand-illusions-impact-of-misperceptions-about-russia-on-u.s.-policy-pub-84845

Saul, John Ralston. 1998. *Reflections of A Siamese Twin: Canada at the Beginning of the Twenty First Century*. Toronto: Penguin Random House Canada.

Senate of Canada. 1970. *Report of the Special Senate Committee on Mass Media*. Ottawa: Government of Canada.

Sherrard, B. undated. "Islam and the Middle East in the American imagination," *Oxford Research Encyclopedia of Religion*: https://oxfordre.com/religion/

Sigler, John H. and Dennis Goresky. 1974. "Public opinion on United States-Canadian relations," *International Organization*, Vol. 28, No. 4, 661–665.

Simpson, Jeffrey. 2000. *Star-Spangled Canadians: Canadians Living the American Dream*. Toronto: HarperCollins.

Skelton, William B. 1994. "High Army leadership in the Era of the War of 1812: The making and remaking of the officer corps," *The William and Mary Quarterly*, Vol. 51, No. 2, 253–274: https://doi.org/10.2307/2946862

Skelton Grant, Judith. 2015. *A Meeting of Minds: The Massey College Story*. Toronto: University of Toronto Press.

Smith, Goldwin. 1891. *Canada and the Canadian Question*. Toronto: Macmillan & Co.

Smith, Joe Patterson. 1933. *The Republican Expansionists of the Early Reconstruction Era*. Chicago: University of Chicago Libraries.

Stanley, George. 1983. *The War of 1812: Land Operations*. Toronto: Gage.

Statistics Canada. 1983. *Historical Statistics*. 2nd ed.: https://www150.statcan.gc.ca/n1/pub/11-516-x/sectiong/4147439-eng.htm

Statistics Canada. 2022. *Foreign Control in the Canadian Economy, 2019*: https://www150.statcan.gc.ca/n1/daily-quotidien/220131/dq220131b-eng.htm

Statistics Canada. n.d. *Estimated Population of Canada, 1605 to Present* (Does not include indigenous persons): https://www150.statcan.gc.ca/n1/pub/98-187-x/4151287-eng.htm

Stern, Robert M., Philip H. Trezise and John Whalley, eds. 1987. *Perspectives on a U.S.-Canadian Free Trade Agreement*. Washington, DC: Brookings Institution.

Stewart, Gordon T. 1992. *The American Response to Canada since 1776*. East Lansing, MI: Michigan State University Press.

Stewart, John. 2010. "Magazines, ministers and "monoculture": The Canada-United States dispute over "split run" magazines in the 1990s," *Canadian Foreign Policy Journal*, Vol. 16, No. 1, 35–48.

Stowe, Harriet Beecher. 1852. *Uncle Tom's Cabin; Or, Life among the Lowly*. Boston: John P. Jewett and Company.

Strate, John and James Sellars. 1993. "Elite opinion on Canada-U.S. Trade liberalization," *American Review of Canadian Studies*, 583–605.

Struck, Doug. 2004. "Forecast frosty for U.S.-Canada ties," *Washington Post*, November 27: www.washingtonpost.com/archive/politics/2004/11/27/forecast-frosty-for-us-canadian-ties/d12875e0-78a8-40e9-80fa-b698b125f603/

Stuart, Reginald. 2007. *Dispersed Relations: Americans and Canadians in Upper North America*. Baltimore: Johns Hopkins University Press.

Stuart, Reginald. 2012. Interview from February 2012, "Dispersed relations: Americans and Canadians in Upper North America," *Interview at Michigan State University*: www.youtube.com/watch?v=sFXgt6E3lxA

Taft, William Howard. 1911a. *Special Message on Canadian Reciprocity*, January 26: www.presidency.ucsb.edu/documents/special-message-canadian-reciprocity

Taft, William Howard. 1911b. *Letter from William H. Taft to Theodore Roosevelt*, January 10: www.theodorerooseveltcenter.org/Research/Digital-Library/Record/ImageViewer?libID=o63302&imageNo=1

Taylor, Alan. n.d. "Uneasy neighbors: Rival political systems in North America," *National Parks Service Series: From the American Revolution to the War of 1812*: www.nps.gov/articles/uneasy-neighbors-1.htm

Taylor, Charles. 1970. *The Pattern of Politics*. Toronto: McClelland & Stewart.

Taylor, Charles. 1992. *Multiculturalism and the Politics of Recognition*. Princeton, NJ: Princeton University Press.

Taylor, Kate. 2014. "'Cansplaining': Why U.S. Media still feels the need to explain Canada to Americans," *Globe and Mail*, October 31: www.theglobeandmail.com/arts/books-and-media/cansplaining-why-us-media-still-feels-the-need-to-explain-canada-to-americans/article21403868/

The Economist. 2021. "Social media are turbocharging the export of America's political culture," *The Economist*, June 12: www.economist.com/international/2021/06/12/social-media-are-turbocharging-the-export-of-americas-political-culture

This American Life. 1997. *Who's Canadian?* May 30: www.thisamericanlife.org/65/whos-canadian

Thoreau, Henry David. 1866. *A Yankee in Canada*. Boston: Ticknor and Fields.

Tocqueville, Alexis de. 1835. *Democracy in America* (Translated by Henry Reeve. Book 1, Chapter XIII). Toronto: Ryerson Press.

Trudeau, Pierre. 1969. *Speech at National Press Club*. Washington, DC.

Truman, Harry S. 1947. *Address before the Canadian Parliament in Ottawa*, June 11: www.trumanlibrary.gov/library/public-papers/111/address-canadian-parliament-ottawa

Tully, James. 1995. *Strange Multiplicity: Constitutionalism in an Age of Diversity*, Cambridge: Cambridge University Press.

Underhill, Frank. 1966. "Foreword," In Peter Russell, ed., *Nationalism in Canada*. Toronto: McGraw-Hill.

United States. 1978. *Perceptions, Relations Between the United States and the Soviet Union*. Washington, DC: Report commissioned by the Senate Committee on Foreign Relations.

United States. 2022. *Direct Investment by Country and Industry, 2021* Bureau of Economic Analysis: www.bea.gov/news/2022/direct-investment-country-and-industry-2021

United States Census Bureau. 2022. *Fourth of July Fun Facts*: www.census.gov/programs-surveys/sis/resources/fun-facts/fourth-of-july.html

Van Alstyne, Richard W. 1952. "Preface to Canada's history," *Current History*, Vol. 135, 280–284: https://doi.org/10.1525/curh.1952.23.135.280

VanNijnatten, D.L. 2006. "Towards cross-border environmental policy spaces in North America: Province-State linkages on the Canada-U.S. Border," *AmeriQuests*, Vol. 3, No. 1.

Vermette, David. 2019. "When an influx of French-Canadian immigrants struck fear into Americans," *Smithsonian Magazine*, August 21: www.smithsonianmag.com/history/french-canadian-immigrants-struck-fear-into-new-england-communities-180972951/

Von Heyking, Amy. 2006. "Talking about Americans: The image of the United States in English-Canadian Schools, 1900–1965," *History of Education Quarterly*, Vol. 46, No. 3, 382–408.

Waite, P.B. 1962. *The Life and Times of Confederation, 1864–1867*. Toronto: University of Toronto Press.

Waite, P.B., ed. 1965. *Pre-Confederation*. Vol. II. Scarborough, ON: Prentice-Hall.

Washington, George. 1775. *Address to the Inhabitants of Canada*, September 14. https://founders.archives.gov/documents/Washington/03-01-02-0358#:~:text=Above%20all%2C%20we%20rejoice%2C%20that,a%20little%20Circle%20of%20Nobility%E2%80%94

Wayland, Sarah V. 1997. "Immigration, multiculturalism and national identity in Canada," *International Journal of Group Rights*, Vol. 5, No. 1, 46–47.

Wilson, Sandy. 1985. *My American Cousin* (Written and directed by Sandy Wilson): https://canfilmday.ca/film/my-american-cousin/

Wiman, Erastus. 1889. "What is the destiny of Canada?" *North American Review*, Vol. 148, No. 391, 665–675.

Winthrop, John. 1630. *A Model of Christian Charity*: https://archive.org/stream/AModelOfChristianCharity/AModelOfChristianCharity_djvu.txt

Wise, S.F. and Robert Craig Brown. 1967. *Canada Views the United States: Nineteenth-Century Political Attitudes*. Seattle: University of Washington Press.

Wiseman, Nelson. 2022. *1950s Canada: Politics and Public Affairs*. Toronto: University of Toronto Press.

Zakaria, Fareed. 2011. *Interview with Charlie Rose*, May 31 (my transcription of an excerpt from that interview): www.charlierose.com

Zimmerman, W. 1977. "The American view of Russia," *The Wilson Quarterly*, Vol. 1, No. 2, 118–128.

Zogby. 2007. *Zogby America, Likely Voters 8/23/07 thru 8/27/07*: www.911truth.org/images/ZogbyPoll2007.pdf

INDEX

Note: Page numbers in *italics* indicate a figure on the corresponding page.

9/11 3–4

Aird, John 112n6
Allen, Cleo Joffrion 78
Allport, Gordon 18
ambivalence, Canadian toward America 37–41
America *see* United States
America, Day by Day (de Beauvoir) 38
American Canadian (newspaper) 28
American Democracy, The (Laski) 38
Americanization of Canada 42
"American Life, This" (radio program) 79
American Response to Canada since 1776, The (Stewart) 20
America the Menace (Duhamel) 38
anglophobia 61
Angus, H.F. 38
annexation: American calls for 71–72, 73; fear of 33, 34, 35–37, 47–51; support for 33, 35
Annexation and Exoneration (Rohmer) 48
anti-Americanism: 1960s and 1970s 43–44; Canadian 20, 22, 23, 25–28, 29, 39, 57n3, 75, 76; economic 96; European 20; French 22; multiculturalism as 46
anti-Canadianism 82
asymmetric interdependence: communication and culture 89–90; cultural nationalism 94–96, 108–9; economic nationalism 96–101; economics 87–88; free trade 101–5, 110; influence of images 108–12; Iraq 105–8, 110–11; one-way mirror 90; security and defense 88–89; US–Canada relations, modern era 90–94
Atwood, Margaret 48, 50, 70–71, 90

Baker, William 40
Ball, George 100
Bancroft, George 66
Bannister, Jennifer 81
Beam, Alex 80
Bélanger, Damien-Claude 27
Belch, Christopher 79
Bengough, J.W.A. *35*
Berger, Carl 75
Berton, Pierre 37–38, 59, 74
Birr, K. 10
borderlands 16–19
Bosnia 106
Boulding, Kenneth 4–5
Bowling for Columbine (movie) 81
Brebner, John Bartlet 28
Bretherton, Cyril Emmanuel 40
Broege, Valerie 48
Brokaw, Tom 80
Brookes, Alan 27
Buchanan, William 8
Buckner, Phillip 69

Bukowczyk, John 18
Bundy, McGeorge 100
Butterworth, William 99

Canada: ambivalence toward America 37–41; American cultural influence on 40–41, 89–90; American image of 58–59, 63–69, 75, 78–80, 84; annexation with the US 33, 34; Canadian studies abroad 15–16; cultural nationalism 94–96, 108–9; culture wars 80–84; economic nationalism 109–10; as friendly neighbor 74–78; image abroad 13–15; immigration promotion 12–14; national image 12–13, 39–40, 101; nationalism 41–45, 75, 76, 89; obsession with United States (*see* Canadian obsession with United States); origins of 23, 24–25; popular images of 78–80; rebellions of 1837–38 31–33, 66, 68–69; as refuge from injustice 69–71; self-image 39, 45, 90–91; as threat to the US 59–63; views on the US 87, 108
Canada and Her Great Neighbor (Angus) 37
Canada–US relations: modern era 90–94; and national images 19–21, 102; post War of Independence 60–62; War of 1812 62; *see also* special relationship
Canadian Citizenship Act 14, 91
Canadian Mosaic (Gibbon) 45
Canadian obsession with United States: ambivalence 37–41; annexation 33–37, 47–51; anti-Americanism 20, 22, 23, 25–28, 29–31; multiculturalism 45; nationalism 41–45; perceptions, early 23–31; perceptions, recent 52–54, 57n10; pro-American sympathies 25, 27, 28–29, 32, 33; reasons for 58; rejection of American model 31–33, 53
Canadian Pacific Railway 14
Cantril, Hadley 8
Caricature History of Canadian Politics, A (Bengough) 35
Carlson, Tucker 82
Carnegie Endowment 75, 77
Carnegie study 37
cartoons, editorial 74
Caves, Richard 97
Cellucci, Paul 1, 107, 111
Cherry, Don 105, 112n10
Chrétien government 1

Chrétien, Jean 105, 106, 111
Clark, Champ 73
Clark, S.D. 37
Cod Fisheries, The (Innis) 75
Cold War 4
Commercial Empire of the St. Lawrence, The (Creighton) 75
Committee for an Independent Canada 43
communication 89–90
confirmation bias 4
Copps, Sheila 95
Corrigan, Patrick *54*
Council of Canadians 50–51
COVID-19 *see* Freedom Convoy
Creighton, Donald 75
Cuban Missile Crisis 76, 89
cultural differences, Canada–US 23–24
cultural diplomacy 15–16
cultural influence 40–41, 89–90
cultural nationalism 94–96, 108–9
culture wars 80–84
Curti, M. 10

Dafoe, John W. 39
Davies, Helen 15
de Beauvoir, Simone 11, 21n5, 38
Declaration of Independence 9, 10, 60
de Vitry, Jacques 21n3
Diefenbaker, John 76, 89, 99
Dispersed Relations (Stuart) 24
Drapeau, Jean 15
Drew, Benjamin 70
Duhamel, Georges 38
Dulles, John Foster 98
durability of images 2–4, 5
Dutil, Patrice 36

economic integration 75–76, 85n9, 87–88, 93
economic nationalism 96–101, 109–10
editorial cartoons 74
European debt crisis 5
Expo 67 15

Fält, Olavi 5
Family Compact 32
film industry 11–12, 38
foreign investment 112n7, 113n14
Foster, Kate 45
France and England in North America (Parkman) 65
Franklin, Benjamin 64
Freedom Convoy 54–55, 82–83

free trade 50–51, 101–5, 110
friendly neighbors 74–78
Frum, David 54
Fulbright Program 10
Fulford, Robert 44

Gibbon, John Murray 45
Glass, Ira 79
golden era 112n4
Gordon Commission 96–97
Gordon, Walter 43, 100
Gotlieb, Allan 44
Grant, George 43, 47, 51
Gravelle, Timothy 18
Great Britain 28, 61–62
Greece 5
Green, Alan G. 28
Greg, Allan 105

Haidt, Jonathan 3
Handmaid's Tale, The (Atwood) 50, 70–71
Harper, Stephen 105
Harrison, Trevor 82
Hart, E.J. 14
Hayward, Victoria 45
Hemingway, Ernest 74
Henry, Patrick 31
Henshaw, Peter 46
Hilling, John *67*
Hollywood 11–12, 38, 89
Homer-Dixon, Thomas 53–54
Horowitz, Daniel 39–40
Horsman, Reginald 34, 62
Howe, Joseph 28–29, 52
Hussein, Saddam 1
Hutchison, Bruce 58

Ignatieff, Michael 105
"I Like Americans" (Hemingway) 74
"I Like Canadians" (Hemingway) 74
images: American images of Canada 58–59, 63–69, 75, 78–80, 84; durability of 2–4, 5; importance of 108–12; policy consequences of 86–87, 91, 93–94; proto-nationalist 29–31; and United States–Canada relations 19–21, 102; *see also* national images
Image, The (Boulding) 5
"Imagining Canada" (documentary) 79
immigration *see* migration
influence: of images 108–12; of the US on Canada 40–41, 55–56, 89–90
Inland Empire 17

Innis, Harold 75
inter-group contact theory 18–19
International Boundary Waters Treaty 36
Intolerable Acts 65
Iran 6, 86
Iraq 1, 105–8, 110–11
Isaacs, Harold 7
"Is Canada Being Americanized?" (Bretherton) 40
Issen, Tajja 52

Jefferson, Thomas 9, 10, 62, 84n2
Joyal, Serge 95

Kennan, George 6–7
Kennedy, John F. 77, 84, 89, 111
Kingwell, Mark 47
Klein, Ralph 105
Klobuchar, Amy 109
Kosovo 106
Kuznets, Simon 97

Lacroix, Patrick 66
Lament for a Nation (Grant) 43, 47
Landon, Fred 57n3
Laski, Harold 38
Latin America 6
Lauck, W. Jett 34
Laurier, Wilfrid 13, 21n6
Lawrence, D.H. 57n7
L'Ennemi américain (Roger) 22
les canadiens 63–67
Lippmann, Walter 5
Lipset, Seymour Martin 22–23
Livingston, Robert 61
L'Obsession anti-américaine (Revel) 22
Locke, John 60, 84n2
"Long Telegram" (Kennan) 7
Lossing, Benson John *63*
Lower, A.R.M. 14
Loyalist Myth 23
Loyalists 24–25

Macdonald Commission 102–3, 110, 112n9
Macdonald, John A. 29–30, 36, 72
Machiavelli, Niccolo 9
MacIver, R.M. 38
MacKay, Robert 31, 32
MacKenzie, David 36
Mackenzie, William Lyon 31, 68–69
MacLennan, Hugh 42
Maltby, Richard 11
Manifest Destiny 69, 72

manufacturing 91
Manulak, Michael 106
Maria Chapdelaine (Hémon) 27
Markovits, Andre 6, 20
Martin, Ged 57n4
Massey Commission 94, 108
McGee, Thomas D'Arcy 29
media: American influence on Canada 40–41; coverage of Canada 78–80; *see also* film industry
melting pot 45
mental territories 17–18
Mercer Report, The (television program) 51
Mercer, Rick 51
Merchant, Livingston 99, 100
Merkel, Angela 5
Michaels, Al 80
migration: Canada–US 26–28; and foreign investment 112n7, 113n14; immigration recruitment 12–13, 68; UK–Canada 28
modern era in US–Canada relations 90–94
Monière, Denis 24
Moodie, Susanna 25
Moore, Michael 81, 85n12
moral superiority 87
Morrissey, Katherine 17–18
Mortimer, Benjamin 68
mosaic 45
movies *see* film industry
Mowat, Farley 42
multiculturalism 45
Murchison, Heather 96
My American Cousin (movie) 48–50, *49*

national images: affective component 20; Canada–United States 1–2, 39–41; cognitive component 20; durability of 2–4, 5; imagining the other 1–8; importance of 8–16; *see also* images
nationalism: cultural 94–96; economic 96–101; "new" Canadian 41–45
Nelles, H.V. 18
New Brunswick 25
Nixon, Richard 92
Nye, Joseph 9

Obama, Barack 81, 86
Oliver, Dean 92
one-way mirror 90
Online News Act, The 109
Ouellet, Fernand 32
Our Canadian Mosaic (Foster) 45

Papineau, Louis-Joseph 32, 66
Paris, Roland 56
Parkman, Francis 65
Paton, Harold S. 36
Patriot Hunters 69
Peace Corps 10
Pearson, Lester B. 98
Peers, Frank 94
Peskin, Lawrence 61
policy consequences of national images 86–87, 91, 93–94
possession fantasies 48
Potter, Evan 16
power, soft 9
pro-American sympathies 25, 27, 28–29, 32, 33
protectionism 72–73
proto-nationalist image 29–31
Public Opinion (Lippmann) 5

Quebec 23, 24, 26, 27, 106–7, 113n12
Quebec Act 64–65

Radio Free Europe 10
Ramirez, Bruno 26
rebellions of 1837–38 31–33, 66, 68–69, 85n5
reciprocity 36, 57n5, 72–73
Reed, Colin 32–33
Reflections of a Siamese Twin (Saul) 46
Refugee, The (Drew) 70
Report of the Royal Commission on Canada's Economic Prospect (Gordon Commission) 96–97
Revel, Jean François 22
Riddell, William 64
Righteous Mind, The (Haidt) 2
Rioux, Jean-Sébastien 107
Robinson, Paul 100, 101
Rogan, Joe 82
Roger, Philippe 22
Rohdie, Sam 21n5
Rohmer, Richard 48
Roman Catholicism 64–65, 66, 84n4
Romantic Canada (Hayward) 45
Roughing It in the Bush (Moodie) 25–26
Royal Commission on National Development in the Arts, Letters, and Sciences (Massey Commission) 94, 108
Royal Commission on the Economic Union and Development Prospects for Canada (Macdonald Commission) 102–3, 110, 112n9

Royal Proclamation of 1763 62
Rumer, Eugene 7
Russia *see* Soviet Union

Sanders, Bernie 81
Sandwell, B.K. 95
Sartre, Jean-Paul 11, 21n5
Saul, John Ralston 46
security and defense 88–89, 91–93
Serbia 106
Sheen, Martin 80
Simpson, Jeffrey 52
Sinclair, Gordon 42
slavery 70, 85n6
Smith, Goldwin 25, 28
soft power 9
Soft Power (Nye) 9
Sokolsky, Richard 7
Soviet Union 6–7
special relationship 7, 78, 92, 93, 112n4
Star-Spangled Canadians (Simpson) 52
stereotypes 7–8, 21n3, 37–41, 87
Stewart, Gordon T. 20, 60, 62, 66
Stewart, John 95
Stowe, Harriet Beecher 70
Stuart, Reginald 24, 26
Suprenant, Lorenzo 27
Surfacing (Atwood) 48

Taft, Robert 73
tariffs 72–73
Taylor, Alan 62, 68
Taylor, Charles 47
Technology and Empire (Grant) 43
Thoreau, Henry David 66
Thucydides 9
trade: asymmetric interdependence 87–88; economic integration 75–76, 77; free trade 50–51, 101–5, 110; importance of 78; in mid-20th century 91; protectionism 72–73; reciprocity 36, 57n5, 72
Trudeau, Justin 81
Trudeau, Pierre 44, 45, 92, 100

Truman, Harry S. 91–92
Trump, Donald 52, 55–56, 82–83
Trumpocracy (Frum) 54

Uncle Tom's Cabin (Stowe) 70, 71, 85n7
Uncouth Nation (Markovits) 6
Underground Railroad 70, 71
Underhill, Frank 41
United Kingdom *see* Great Britain
United States: Canadian obsession with (*see* Canadian obsession with United States); Canadian views on 37–41, 87, 93–94 (*see also* anti-Americanism, Canadian); decline of 52–54, 55; entertainment industry 11–12, 38; image abroad 10–12, 86–87; proto-nationalist image 29–31; self-image 9–11; stereotypes of 37–41; views on Canada 58–59, 63–69, 75, 78–80, 84, 101, 108, 109; views on English Canada 68; views on *les canadiens* 63–67
United States–Canada relations: modern era 90–94; and national images 19–21, 102; post War of Independence 60–62; War of 1812 62; *see also* special relationship
United States Information Agency 10
Unknown Country, The (Hutchinson) 58–59

Van Alstyne, Richard W. 14
Vietnam 44, 70
Voice of America 10
Von Heyking, Amy 38–39

Waite, P.B. 24, 25, 29
Walsh, Liam 3
War of 1812 62–63
War of Independence 2
Washington, George 64
"Who's Canadian?" (radio program) 79–80
Why We Act Like Canadians (Berton) 59
Winslow, Edward 25
Winthrop, John 9
Wise, S.F. 25, 30–31

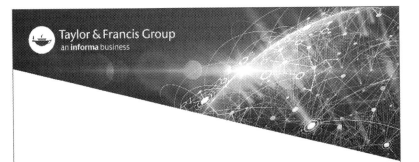

Printed in the United States
by Baker & Taylor Publisher Services